WATCH OUT LADIES

15 THINGS EVERY WOMAN WHO'S LOOKING FOR LOVE NEEDS TO BE WARNED ABOUT

TO PROTECT HER HEART, BODY,
FIND TRUE LOVE & AVOID A
LIFETIME OF LONELINESS

BART SMITH

COPYRIGHT NOTICE

Watchoutladies.com
FindTheOneForMe.com
RelationshipRegrets.com
LawsOfTheBedroom.com
BartSmithBooks.com
BartsCookies.com

TABLE OF CONTENTS

INTRODUCTION

Why Warn Women To "WATCH OUT?"

Here's why ... For the past 30+ years, there has been a quiet, undisputed international crisis going on in the hearts of women all over the world. This crisis will only get worse if WOMEN don't put an end to it. That's right, women (with men's help). What's going on? Millions more women are continuing to enter their 30s and 40s SINGLE, UNWED, and WITHOUT CHILDREN. If you are a woman reading this, can you relate? If you haven't entered your 30s or 40s yet, does this reality for millions of other women frighten you? It should. It better. Do you know women who can relate to this lonely reality?

For MILLIONS of other women that can't relate to what you just read, perhaps this does: STILL dating, got PREGNANT (out of wedlock or with the wrong man), got married (then divorced), now single (again) trying to navigate a world that isn't overflowing with the kind of REAL LOVE your heart longs for? Just go on any dating website and read over a few thousand female profiles looking for a man and love in today's world. I have. You might find they read like this:

"**I've been alone and single for too long.** I'm looking for an honest man with ambition and who likes to be romantic. I never tell lies because I don't like liars. I'm also hoping he is funny so we can laugh a lot together. I hope you are sincere, caring, loving, intelligent, affectionate and passionate. I will wait for your letter. **Will you comfort my tiny broken heart?**"

"I am looking for a sincere, romantic man to love and be loved. What is your idea of romance? My idea of romance is growing old together. Please contact me if that describes you. I want to find my Mr. Right here to build a beautiful home together. **Let's start our own love story.** I'm looking for a man who is loyal, gentle, easy-going, loving and caring. He must be considerate, a gentleman and knows how to treat a lady like a lady. **He must want to build a warm family with me.** I am not a picky woman, I just want to find someone who will love and cherish me as I will him. He should also be hard working. **We will build the sweetest family together** and I will make him the happiest man in the world."

"**I have been divorced for three years already. My last marriage was bad. I found my ex-husband with another woman in bed.** That's why I divorced him. I can't stand cheating. Please, read this! I am not seeking a man who acts like an 18 year old. He and I would have nothing in common, because my heart is much older than my age. If I have described you and you choose to write, I will certainly respond. **I am seeking a man who is looking for a serious relationship and won't play games.** He should care about his health and fitness. I do. We can stay fit together. It doesn't matter if he is a little overweight, I will take good care of him. Height, weight, again, not a problem with me. I care most about what's inside and not what's outside. Beyond that, thank you, for reading my profile. Let's start a conversation about love and our potential lives together."

"While money is important, if you have a reliable income, as do I, **it's not how much you earn but how you will treat me.** I do not wish for expensive things. If we have to live on a budget, we will because it's the right thing. **The main qualities I look for in a man are trust, caring and does he want to be a husband and make me his wife.** I am dreaming about a reliable man with whom I will build a cozy home and a happy family. I want to have two (or more) children and I am sure they will be as talented as their parents. Do you agree?"

"I am looking for my soulmate on this website who is honest, loyal, truthful and caring. I want to share my life with him. **I want a man who doesn't mind sitting on a beach with me anywhere and wishing upon a star.** I know we are both looking for our life mate. We both hope that we will have a warm and harmonious family in the near future, to experience and share the happiness and sadness, and to love each other wholeheartedly forever. Are you the man who is willing to do these things with me? If so, **I cannot wait to be held in your arms forever.**"

"I know exactly what I want from life. **I dream to meet my man and love him until my last breath.** I am so tired of being alone and solving the problems of life by myself. I need the strong shoulder of my man to rest my head on. Where are you?"

"I want to find the one and only man for me for life! I believe that the right man will not want other women and will love only me. Unfortunately, **I see so many guys my age are not true** and cannot stop wanting to be with every woman."

"**I am not young any more, even though I do not look my age.** I am seeking a man who can be my true love. I wish I can find a man who wants to get married. I wish to spend the rest of my life with him. **I hate the feeling of being alone.** I hope he is considerate, caring, responsible, has a sense of humor, and wants to **build a family**. If you also have the same dream like me, then please inquire about my inner beauty or you will miss me. I'm ready to be a wife and a mother. I'm really ready for it!"

Wow, how did you feel after reading just a few of those female profiles looking for love? Sure, many of them read very similarly, but did you catch the many different (but common) hurts, wants, wishes, concerns and worries they all expressed? Can you relate in any way, shape or form to what those women want out of life and finding their soulmate to love and be loved forever? Here's another woman and what she wrote on a dating website just as I wrote the WARNING intro section. I paraphrase for brevity ...

> "... I am serious to find my love here and I don't want to play games. Time is limited. I want to enjoy life with my man and I hope I can find you as soon as possible and start our new life together. Time is running out for us!"

Ladies, I have written many books on relationships for many reasons. First, and foremost, I'm a romantic at heart. I also like to write. I also believe in love and finding the love of your life and living happily ever after. "*I do!*" See? There, I said it! HA-HA.

All kidding aside, I am also different from you, being a man, and you a woman. Yes, there are differences in the genders. Don't let anyone try to convince you otherwise. I say that because, as a man, we (men) don't have the same set of worries, concerns, fears and time lines as women do with their lives, hearts and bodies as you do. For example, and there are many, men don't worry about *CARRYING* the baby. Men just have a co-role in *MAKING IT* and at *ALMOST* any age! We can also marry a younger woman if we want to start a family, as many women are fine with marrying a man 10-15 years older than her if he can provide adequately, financially speaking, of course. While men should also consider the health risks of making babies when they're 40-50 years old or older, women should be concerned about carrying their first baby in their 30s and 40s due to health risks related to the baby and themselves. What's more, do you want to turn 60 when your first child enters

HIGH SCHOOL as a FRESHMAN? How about turning 70 when your last child graduates college? YIKES! A female friend of mine told me when she had her son at 42 years old, she never would have seen the day when his friends mistakenly referred to her as his grandmother when she dropped him off at school one day. My heart sank for her as she shared her sad, revealing story. Now, don't get me wrong. The birth of any child is a gift to be celebrated. HIS/HER life has just begun and I know you'll make a great mom. Right? Of course, you will. Even though I could give more examples how men and women are different, let's get back to the book. Women's HEARTS (and their love lives) are suffering NOW and for FAR TOO LONG. Allow me to get right to it ... the TOP 15 REASONS why women, especially, need to WATCH OUT in the world of love, dating, relationships, marriage, sex, having babies, choosing and keeping a good guy around and not rejecting him for the little things while she opts to trade up for Mr. Perfect who ... DOESN'T EXIST!

Really quick, what about the guys? Don't they have to watch out too? Sure, but in different ways. After you look over the table of contents for this book, I think you'll agree NONE of the 15 THINGS women need to watch out for really relate to guys. That said, I did write LAWS OF THE BEDROOM: What Women Want From Men Inside & Outside Of The Bedroom for guys to help keep us in line with making you happy for the rest of our lives. So, the guys aren't off the hook.

After you read WATCH OUT LADIES and/or listen to it in audio format, I hope it helps ensure that you have the best chance at finding love quickly and confidently in, what I feel, is a messed up world out there when it comes to finding love, let alone, a love that lasts. Again, this book is NOT for men. It is for WOMEN who want to find a good man to live with and marry SOONER than LATER!

Here is a quick note as to how this book was written. It isn't written like a novel or a series of stories. No. From my observations, we don't have time for that. I wrote it so you could read it quickly and

get busy finding love fast once you've digested much of the advice I recommend. Just open the book anywhere, focus your eyes on what you are about to read and start learning! In advance, I hope this book really does help. If it does, please, feel free to reach out to me and let me know. I'd love to hear that there's one more lady out there who's found her man and is on her way to living life filled with love and all she's ever dreamed of ...

FOR NAYSAYERS

BE FOREWARNED you are very brave, courageous, even rebellious (in a good way) to consider reading this book and potentially following what you will read. Why? Because it has your best interest at heart in a world that doesn't care so much about ... YOUR HEART! I say this because there will be people, organizations, peers, institutions, friends, certain feminists, even some males who do not want you to follow what's prescribed among these pages.

In fact, they will do everything they can to discredit what you will read, even to the extent of publicly bad-mouthing or even bullying you (or me) into dismissing any common sense advice that makes "good sense" to you from what this book has to offer. Why so? Because they have an agenda, plain and simple. Whether it's political, financial, cultural, social, media/pop culture related, or just pure evil all around. Make no mistake about it, these people will lie to you, fabricate the truth, stretch your faith and try to make you cave under their *pressures*. You may fall prey to their bidding, financial gain, mind control, you name it. If you don't believe me, just observe their behavior, tone and words.

Someone who does have your best interest at heart will say nothing (but praise) for what's inside this book, move on and then let you be. Those with ill intentions will get upset, throw tantrums, display hostile like disapproval or disgust (against what's good for you) publicly so you feel badly and cave to their B.S. It's that simple. Besides, in a FREE COUNTRY, don't you have a right to be good to yourself? Don't you have the right to do what you think is best for your mind, heart, body and soul? Or does someone want to steal your soul away? Uh, yeah, duh! Well, to heck with the naysayers, I say. Your LIFE, HEART and present/future MEMORIES are at stake. For example, if you ever hear some of the following statements, CONFIDENTLY IGNORE THEM and walk away:

- **You can be promiscuous and have sex just like a man** and be free of guilt, depression and/or life altering consequences. = THAT'S **B.S.**

- **We're all sexual creatures** and can behave like animals if we *feel* like it. It's about *feelings* and not logic! Gender is fluid. = THAT'S **B.S.**

- **You have all the time in the world to get married**. Pursue your career full-time until you're 30-35 then settle down. = THAT'S **B.S.**

- **Living together** will help encourage him to marry me. = THAT'S **B.S.**

- **"I'm female, perfect, entitled, young and beautiful.** It's the man who has to bend over backwards for me. I have a long checklist of criteria for him to meet if I'm going to be with him. I also don't need to learn how to cook for him, my children, myself or bring anything to the relationship except my v*****." = 100% GRADE "A" **B.S.**

Remember these are lies with the intentions of hurting your heart and present/future love life. They all lead to LONELINESS and HEARTACHE. Instead, (1) Focus on what's important to YOU and for YOUR life and not anyone else's. (2) Do the right thing. It pays dividends in the long run. (3) At the end of the day, you have to live with yourself and the decisions you made (good/bad). Nobody owns you or your mind. Only you can let them control you. DON'T! Those who approve of this book want what's best for you. Side with them and PURSUE LOVE FOREVER.

SEX: Too Soon
& Too Much
... and without a ring!

Hey ladies, are you the type of woman to sleep around? You probably don't sleep around, but I'm sure some of you have gone to bed "too soon" with a guy either on the first or second date or maybe within a week or two of meeting someone you liked physically or were attracted to. What's the harm? That's okay, right? Well, why did you sleep with him so quickly? Was it because:

1. **You slept with him because you got caught up in the moment.** Now that the moment's gone, what are you left with? A memory? A longing to be with him? More than anything, you're left with nothing, but a moment's memory. Gone like the wind.

2. **You slept with him because you were lonely.** Did he stick around after the deed? Did you wind up lonely again because

he never called you back or wanted to see you again? Did he start ghosting you after what you thought were close and intimate moments together? Probably. Most likely. No? Yeah?

3. **You used sex for leverage or revenge or to rebound from your last bad relationship.** Did that night of rebound sex cure your relationship blues? What you never saw coming was this new lingering memory on your mind that you can try, but not erase from your mind. No doubt, if you don't want to spend time with that dude, you had revenge sex. What is he wants to see you again. Now, you have more new problems to deal with. You can just imagine, I'm sure.

4. **You felt pressured. Doesn't no mean no?** Instead, you could have taken the heat, been a prude, only to wake up the next morning in your own bed (alone) and smiling because you didn't do it. Sure he called you names, but sticks and stones, right? Names will never hurt you? Name-calling fades quickly and are light on the soul to bare. Sexual memories and the exchanging of fluids in an intimate night of passion do not fade so fast. It can take YEARS for them to be replaced by better episodes, hopefully, that include LOVE in the sexual equation.

5. **You thought it could lead to a long-term relationship.** How many of those one-night stand hook-ups ever result in one of those? Uh, none. Okay, maybe one. No? None? Okay, back to ZERO.

6. **You thought sexual chemistry would translate into a stunning, wonderful and gorgeous personality.** Little did you know, the man you physically merged with last night turned out to be a substance and/or woman abuser.

7. **Believed you could have a no-strings-attached**

relationship (i.e., friends with benefits). How'd that turn out? You now want to see him on a regular basis, like boyfriend/girlfriend, and he doesn't. He's got another one-nighter lined up and doesn't want to take your calls. How's that make you feel?

8. **You slept with him only hoping he would LOVE you and marry you eventually.** You didn't move in together, did you? You did? Oh, no! How'd that turn out? He said he'd marry you within six months. You're on month four living together. Any plans made yet? How about a promise ring? No sign of either?

9. **You thought you could keep him close to you, to get to know you, if you just let him have sex with you sooner than later.** How'd that approach work? Men usually want sex to satisfy an immediate gratification or urge. If you want him for the long run, see if he'll stick around without having sex too soon. Sure, kiss, pet, play, but no sex. Besides, after the deed is done, where does he go? Leave you to go back to his place (or you leave his place) or stick around (because you're in a relationship headed towards something bigger/better for your finger? Which would you prefer?

10. **You slept with him solely because he was HOT! That's good enough, right? Maybe ... NOT!** Hot or not, sleeping with anyone too soon can cause YOU the same mental, emotional and physical repercussions whether you slept with someone or not. What happens AFTER the event is where the trouble starts ... IF ... he doesn't stick around. Oh, but he was HOT. Yeah, sure. Tell that to your heart when it longs for his touch at night and he ain't there. He's with, uh, someone else tonight. Sounds like that HOT GUY just turned oh, so cold!!!

Have I missed any reason why you'd sleep with a man too soon? If so, you know what they are like and can do to your own inward reflection about why you shouldn't have. Hindsight is 20/20. I know.

So, what do you think about this list? Can you relate to anything mentioned? Guys too can relate to many of them and are least guilty of perpetuating a few on to you, the gal. While it's not easy to get over sleeping with someone who doesn't return your phone call or ask for a next date or even show interest in starting a relationship with you, IT'S BEST to learn from this list, memorize it, live by it and never make these mistakes (about having sex too soon) again with any man.

What is the magic amount of time you should wait to have sex with someone? It depends. On what? For starters:

MINORS: If you're under 18 and having sex and you're caught, you should be charged a $500-$1,000 fine for each offense and sent to detention at school for a month. Parents should have some responsibility in this, but for the kids, they too must see the error of their ways and have some skin in the game when it comes to punishment. So, for example, if they were in junior high (6-8th grade), I'd ground them for a year. Talk to them before they act, so they know the consequences. Also, because they're getting older and dabbling in sexual/adult-like activities, their mother and I would take them down to juvenile hall (i.e., kid jail) to see where they'd spend the night or a week if they were convicted of having sex with a minor, which is a statutory crime. If the parents have a choice of not of sending them to juvenile hall for a period of time, I would tell my son/daughter, "Yes, you will do time for the crime." Done. I think they'd behave a little better if they knew they'd have that on their record. C'mon, mistakes (i.e., teen pregnancies) cost everyone time, money, investment, resources, reputation, etc. Don't you think it's worth it to instill a little fear into these young minds? I think so. Better to be preventive than reactionary after the deed can't be undone. Personally, I'd see if I could rent a jail cell for the night and leave them there. (HAHA, NOT KIDDING!) Maybe I'd leave them there for the whole weekend. If caught, I'd have them write a five-page letter to the parents of the minor they had sex with. Among other things I'd do to them ... Call me and I'll give you 10 more things you can add to this list already. My kids are not going to have sex. While I can't control them, for sure, I can still bring to their attention the severity of the act they're messing with = MINORS HAVING SEX SHOULD BE AGAINST THE LAW.

If they were almost or more than 16 years old, I'd take away their right to drive until they graduated high school. Sure, they can drive us parents to the grocery store or to get gas for the car, but not alone and NO FUN DRIVING ALONE WITH FRIENDS to the local mall, school or hangout joint. They can also kiss their weekends goodbye for six months. I'd tell my kids each year as they enter another year of high school until they graduate and summer vacation, "Have sex, and I find out, I will make your life a living Hell. Did I say, 'I love you?' There, I said it. I do, really. You know that. BUT SERIOUSLY, YOU ARE MINORS. Have sex; go to jail. Also, if you or someone you have sex with gets pregnant, I'm charging you for every dime I spend to pay for THAT financial mistake. Know this, you cannot have sex unless there are two factors involved: (1) You have a JOB to pay for the baby. Uh, you don't. So? No sex. (2) You have the means to take care of a baby, such as, you have your own home. Uh, you don't! So, no sex. (3) You're in LOVE. Dating a teenager is not love. He/she is just LEARNING about life. So, I go back to #1 and #2, which you have neither. So? No sex. Got it? I'll be watching you guys all throughout your school years. Now, I love you. This meeting is over unless you have any questions, which I'm happy to hear and discuss. You're my children and I love you. Who wants to go first? No question is dumb. It's only dumb if you don't ask it. Better to ask it here, now, when you're safe and in the clear versus when you're in trouble, hiding something, and afraid to share the bad news with anyone."

ADULTS: This is a tricky one because I'm not going to turn preacher on you, but I will say this ... Don't have sex with anyone, unless #1) you're BOTH employed and have your own money/savings (usually from stable jobs/careers); #2) you're in love with each other and/or could say, (HER) "You know, if he got me pregnant, I could marry him right now." Guys should be able to say the same thing. (HIM) "If I got her pregnant, I could see myself marrying her. I LOVE her. It's great to finally find the one." There. It's very simple and to the point. ONE RULE = LOVE & MONEY. Both components can be used to SUPPORT the couple and their baby on the way or the deep-rooted emotions they'll stir up inside each other. If LOVE isn't there, just LUST, then you shouldn't be there having sex. Go ahead if you want to, but remember the aftermath of emotions and cravings you'll have. Is it worth it? Nine times out of ten, NO. I think that's fair to say, right? LOVE+INCOME will give you both what it takes to be able to make the hard and mature decisions in the moment when mature adult thinking counts. Other than that, depending your age and your relationship goals, you're wise enough to or not to have sex when you want and with whom.

How long should you wait to sleep with a man? Long enough in order to find out:

1. **Does he like you for who you are as a person or is he using you for his own personal gratification?** Ask yourself, "What do I get out of this night?" Have you given him enough time to see if he runs from your personality? Do you drive him away with how you act, behave, talk, etc.? If so, and he does go away, aren't you glad you didn't have

sex with him? If you did, he'd be on your mind and he ain't around. That's not good.

2. Does he like hanging out with you more than his friends? If he does, then this guy is a close keeper and sex will be great because he likes hanging around you. That's what couples and married folk are like. They hang around each other after sex.

3. Can he see that being with you for the long run is something he'd like to do with you? What about you? If you both see long-term potential, and you're close to committing to each other, sex then is a good thing between two people.

4. Does he want to have kids and with you! It's all the more reason to talk long-term plans and consider sex a safe go ahead to bond your love tighter and together.

5. On the flip side, does he have any (bad) habits, traits, addictions or behaviors that are a no-go and you should RUN for your life from him. Wow, aren't you glad you didn't sleep with him? I'm just saying, but if a man drinks a lot, or shows any sign of verbal or other kind of abuse, then you're only seeing the tip of the iceberg. Do not date, marry or try to change him. You're not his therapist. RUN! If he shows impatience and is mean to you in his tone or pushy (wanting sex with you) – then those are bad character signs, sister. RUN! Fake some kind of female health crisis, then make like a shepherd and get the flock out of there!!!

You know, I have a saying, "If he's not willing to put a ring on your finger, then don't let him put his finger into your ring." I'll let you figure out that innuendo for yourself, but think about that. You've got the prize he wants, make him earn it. If not, he won't and he'll leave you for the next freebie that comes around.

BOOKS I RECOMMEND YOU READ AFTER MINE

Sex & The Soul Of A Woman: The Reality of Love & Romance In An Age Of Casual Sex

by Paula Rinehart

Having Sex, Wanting Intimacy: Why Women Settle For One-Sided Relationships

by Jill P. Weber

Boundaries in Dating: How Healthy Choices Grow Healthy Relationships

by Henry Cloud

Prude: How The Sex-Obsessed Culture Damages Girls & America Too

by Carol Platt Liebau

Sex With Multiple Men
... and for too many years!

What about sleeping with too many men? Count how many men you've slept with. Is it under 5? More than 5? More than 10? Remember the expression "quality over quantity?" Think about that as you look back on your life and going forward into your future. As women reach their late 20s on into their 30s, the notion of quality starts to replace quantity of hot studs and bad boys. Problem ... Is it too late for you to find a quality good guy to accomplish your motherhood and matrimonial goals?

Heading into the future (STARTING NOW) with a new outlook on dating, your sex life, and marriage, some day, think QUALITY over QUANTITY. It's like choosing LOVE over LUST. Spiritual feelings over falling for fleshly desires that only leave you feeling EMPTY. Look for LOVE in a man.

Look for a man who will LOVE you, stand by you, and even support you. I know, he's hot and you want to jump him. Well, control yourself, for the sake of your heart tomorrow morning and the months that follow.

DOWNSIDES OF TOO MUCH SEX, WITH TOO MANY MEN & FOR TOO MANY YEARS

Despite what you might hear from sexual enthusiasts (i.e., corrupters of your mind/heart/soul) or read online about we're all sexual creatures, have fun, go for it, you deserve it, your body is hot, nothing could go wrong, it's just one night ... All of that talk is pure B.S. Whether these deniers of reality want to come off as cool, hip, trendy, liberated, independent, powerful, strong, acting "man-like" or whatever type of B.S. they're coming up with, in the end, you're the one who will always get hurt the most. Not the guy. Although, guys do have feelings too and have their own issues to deal with when having sex with too many women as well. This book, though, is about you. So, let's take a dive into the pool of REALITY and what can happen to you if you have too much sex with TOO MANY MEN.

GETTING HURT: When women have sex, they (can) fall in love with the man they're with when maybe they shouldn't BE WITH HIM in the first place! Are you married to him, dating him or did you find him sitting next to you at the bar last night? If you don't know him, he could be a total loser, abuser, con man, ex-con, you name it. Get to know him first before you let him touch your pink surprise or rolling hills of bountiful joy. Another thing, you can't put a condom on your heart to protect it from getting hurt. Try it. It won't work. So, you have to be selective and careful who you sleep with.

BONDING BLUES: Sex is the glue that holds relationships together. After sex, while men are ready to get back to their day/night, women tend to want to cuddle. If you don't have the relationship to start with, the glue (to bond) does you no good, but makes a mess all over the floor, table, counter, etc. THINK RELATIONSHIP FIRST, SEX SECOND. This way, the bond will be there along with the cuddling, because you're in a relationship. Bond with someone you know will stick around. Get to know him first. Don't set yourself up to bond with that body pillow again and again, because you had sex with too many men too soon and they all LEFT YOU because they weren't in a relationship with you.

DISEASES: Sex with too many men opens the door to too many opportunities to contract some kind of sexually transmitted disease (STD). A friend of mine told me that a lot of the men she's been dating recently turned out to be bisexual. You know what that means, right? Yep, gay sex brings those bareback diseases home to a vagina (or other holes). Did you know women are more susceptible to contracting sexually transmitted diseases than men? Great, all she needs is for that bi-guy to have 50+ sexual partners (in his lifetime; men love sex, remember) in order to catch something and then say, "Bi-Bi, (bye-bye) have a nice diseased life." That's just great. Trouble is? She wouldn't even know it. When he/she eventually breaks up, she's got a nice gift left behind from him that she can't get rid of. You know many homosexuals do not tell others about their diseases even though there are laws on the books that tell them they are required to? Why so? For many evil reasons, they don't tell. So? The woman gets screwed and not in the right way. Now, the guy doesn't have to be bisexual to bring home diseases. If he sleeps around enough, he's bound to pick up something as well. So, #1) get in a relationship first, #2) get tested, #3) then have sex. Waiting for the test results to come back can actually build up the fun to jump each other when you're in the clear or the opposite will serve you both if you find out one (or both) of you does have something. Whew, a week's worth (or more) of waiting saved one or both of you years of torment living with an STIs, in particular HIV/AIDS, human papillomavirus (HPV), syphilis, Chlamydia, cervical cancers and other diseases all due to risky sexual behaviors with multiple men, whether straight, bi or homosexual. The costs of STIs and these diseases are enormous, not just for women, but on society as a whole.

STALKERS: Not that men are going to stalk you physically for another roll in the hay, some might, but they will be thinking about you and the great time they had with you. To me, that's mental stalking, because they weren't invited back into your life to stay awhile. You might be trying to get them out of your mind, but they won't and don't want to in some cases. Then, one day, when they're lonely, thirsty for some action, without a girlfriend/wife to relieve them, and they see you on some social media website, they just might reach out to you, again. They could even send you a text too, "Hey, what are you doing tonight? This weekend? I loved the time we spent together. Wanna meet up?" You know what they want. NOTE TO SELF: "If you didn't have sex with them in the first place, you wouldn't be experiencing these types of advances and unwanted contacts." So, for the sake of minimizing future interactions with guys who only want one thing, don't give it to them in the first place. Again, look for LOVE in a guy. Look for ROMANCE in a guy. Look for RELIABILITY in a guy. Go for those things first. Sex always comes with a relationship, for the most part. Don't put the cart before the horse. Relationship first, sex second. Remember that. Live it. Don't let anyone convince you otherwise. They don't have to live with the guilt, ill feelings, heartache, pregnancy (with a bad dude) and pain you might feel after another wrong romp in the hay goes astray.

UNPLEASANT MEMORIES YOU CAN'T ERASE: Here's one for you. I have a saying that goes like this, "You cannot reformat your brain like you can a computer hard drive." You know what that means, right, to format a hard drive? It means to completely erase what's on that drive so you can start over with a fresh, clean, new start. When you have sex with anyone, no matter how long ago it was, years can pass, and you'll still remember little details about those sexual episodes of your life. What's wrong with that? Well, when you finally do meet the love of your life, depending on how many men you slept with (either) you won't be able to get them out of your mind or thoughts of the one for you will be clouded by memories of the sexual episodes of your past. Not that they will override your chosen one, but you get the idea. Just try minimizing the quantity you sleep with and go for quality. Specifically, as few as possible on up to when you meet THE ONE.

REPRODUCTIVE RISK FACTORS & FERTILITY DEMISE: How does not being able to have a baby 5-15 years down the road make you feel if you sleep around too much, with too many men, and for multiple years? It can happen. If the previous reasons to minimize a woman's promiscuity didn't move you, maybe this should. Studies have concluded, where reproductive health matters of women who have multiple sexual partners are concerned, women should not be sleeping around and should be more selective with whom they share a bed with; preferably, a husband, steady boyfriend, fiancé, etc. The more sexual partners you have, the greater your risk for sexually transmitted diseases (STDs) like HIV/AIDS and other life-threatening conditions, such as prostate cancer, oral cancer and cervical cancer. Sounds good so far, right? NOT! Chlamydia and gonorrhea are preventable causes of pelvic inflammatory disease (PID) and infertility. If untreated, a certain percentage of women with Chlamydia go on to develop PID. Chlamydia can cause fallopian tube infection without any symptoms. YIKES! The silent killer of baby-making potential! PID and (silent) infection in the upper genital tract can also cause permanent damage to the fallopian tubes, uterus, and surrounding tissues, which all leads to infertility. GREAT! All that sexual fun over the years with multiple men and now you pay the price … you can't have a baby! Even if the odds are 25-50% it won't happen to you, would you really want to play Russian Roulette with your body like that? I wouldn't and I'm a dude. And as a dude, I wouldn't want to know my gal was sleeping around with 10+ men over the last 10-15 years of her life.

While I could come up with more DOWNSIDES to sleeping around with too many men and for too many years, are these good enough to take a second look at your love life and the decisions you'll make going forward? I want you to WATCH OUT and, as best you can, save yourself for your one true love. Real quick, here's a bonus. Did you know a woman's body may incorporate DNA from the semen of casual sex partners? Hmm, how does that sit with you? What did they say about alcoholism and abuse running in the genes of some people's families? Is that bad boy a drunk? Got rage issues? Do the math, ladies, and remove yourself away from these situations.

One quick story before we get into the UPSIDES of not sleeping around or even moving in with too many men ... I was talking to a beautiful young lady, about 29 years old, who told me she just moved in with her boyfriend. I asked her if she'd live with other boyfriends before. She said, "Yes, two others." I replied, "When will you stop giving these boys what they want (sex) and get a ring on that finger from one of them?" She stopped in her tracks and said, "I don't know. You're right." I replied, "Think about it. You're 29 now. For 10 years past you've been giving men what they want, what are you getting out of the exchange or is it a one-way arrangement? They win and you lose? Make this your last move-in situation (and marry him) or get out while you still can. Time is not on your side at 29. The next man you move in with should be your husband." She got out of her car, gave me a hug and thanked me with a small tear in her eye. Who knows what the past 10 years of dating has been like for her. I must have struck a chord by something I said. Ladies, WATCH OUT for YOU! No one else will, except me, but I'm over here and you're over there and all you have is this book (or audio) to be your friend/guide. That's a great first step forward, I think.

UPSIDES TO HAVING LITTLE TO NO SEX & WITH FEWER MEN

SAFEGUARDING YOUR BABY-MAKING POTENTIAL/FERTILITY: This should be your #1 priority. You know why now based on the last (DOWNSIDES) section. Enough said here. Do the math and start making decisions that protect your baby-making potential. Stop sleeping around and for so long with too many men. The same goes for the pill and certain female contraceptives if taken for long periods of time (like 10+ years). Recent studies prove birth control can increase a woman's risk of breast cancer by up to 38%, depending on how long she has taken the pill. The risk is associated with all forms of hormonal contraception, such as the pill, injections or IUDs, when compared with women who have NEVER used them. IDEA: Get off these if you can/choose, focus on finding your one true man, and keep yourself clean for makin' your babies with him.

NO B.S. OR OTHER UNWANTED DRAMA IN YOUR LIFE: Another big plus to not sleeping around is you avoid all the drama and B.S. that's associated with having sex with multiple men over the years.

NO GUILT, HEARTACHE, WORRY, STRESS, CONCERNS: No one likes guilt, heartache, worry, stress or concerns either. Stop having promiscuous/hook-up sex and you'll rid yourself of these unhealthy emotions as well.

FOCUSED ENERGY, VITALITY AND CONCENTRATION: Without drama in your life, you acquire clear focus, unlimited energy and concentration to get done what needs to be done, whether it's finishing school, kick-starting a new career or pushing your current one where you want him to go. You might not know this, but successful male athletes abstain from sex and masturbation during their training months right up to their event.

MORE RESPECT FOR YOURSELF & FUTURE HUSBAND: For many, there's meaning and value in saving yourself (as best you can) for that special someone you eventually end up with. Nobody is perfect and we all love sex, at least most of us. Still, it is best to think QUALITY over QUANTITY and go for the quality guy with the most long-term value. Don't let your guard down. Don't give in to pressure. Rise to the occasion and show your true strength. NO! Feelings of rejection fade within 24-48 hours. Memories of doing whatever you did with him last forever. How many forevers will you have on your mind when you finally meet the man who walks you down the aisle? Those feelings fade and you don't have the memories of seeing that person naked. There's no obligation to call them or go back and see them or take their calls. You didn't take it that far. Sleep with them, as in, FALL ASLEEP in each other's arms. JUST DON'T *DO IT!* You'll feel better about yourself in the morning.

Remember the scene in the movie, *Don Juan Demarco*, with Johnny Dep and Marlon Brando? There was a scene with Don Juan and his love, Doña Ana, on the beach. She asked him, *"I will accept that I am not the first, if you will tell me with the same honesty. How many others have there been?"* His response? *"This would have been a very good time for me to lie! ... Including you, there have been ... exactly ... 1,502. I could see that this was a sum substantially greater than the one she had in mind, and not easy for her to assimilate. Try as she might."* (See this scene at TinyURL.com/donjuan1502)

Is that bad? Why is that not good? Well, when you do find the love of your life, who else is on your brain when you're naked? Maybe, some of those other guys! Suppose you slept with 20 men in your life. How special will THE ONE be when you meet him if he finds out he's #21 on your list of poles you've danced around. The same goes for guys. They're not off the hook either. The fewer sexual partners for everyone the better.

MEN ACTUALLY START BEHAVING BETTER BECAUSE YOU DO: Ladies, in certain ways YOU really do control men's behavior (more than they do) by #1) insisting they behave like gentlemen and #2) by acting more feminine and lady-like. If you don't go that route and demand more from men (on a good behavior-level), then the reverse will unfold. When you lower your standards and act like the pigs men can be (i.e., smokin', drinkin', swearin', sex all over the place, etc.), then guys will act like pigs too because YOU let them get away with it. When that happens, we all wind up in the mud and not lovin' life.

With so many more upsides that I'm sure you can think of, make a list of them and read them every day. Try making a list of 10 good reasons to slow your sex life down some, focusing on your passions and finding LOVE.

BOOKS I RECOMMEND YOU READ AFTER MINE

Unhooked: How Young Women Pursue Sex, Delay Love and Lose at Both

Laura Sessions Stepp

Single Woman Seeks Perfect Man, Facing the Consequences Of Unhealthy Relationships

by Dani Miser

Pregnant, Unmarried
& With The Wrong Guy
(A Recipe For Heartache)

We can all agree, it's easier to PREVENT something going into the future than it is to UNDO something in the past that you regret happened and now you have to LIVE WITH IT for the REST OF YOUR LIFE.

DON'T MAKE THE SAME MISTAKE MILLIONS of other women have made and sleep with the wrong guy, get pregnant, and now what? You're not available to meet that nicer guy down the road or finish school or pursue that dream job opportunity. What's more? You're really not the catch you once were when you were single (without kids). HE wanted to make you a mamma, but someone beat him to it. So, he's moved on.

What's more? No (nice) guy is going to want to bail you out and pay for your mistake in choosing to cock ride the bad boy when you could have had both, the ride and the nice guy. But, like men, you were thinking with the brain between your legs rather than the one upstairs. I know, it sounds crude, but isn't it the truth? Guys are accused of this all the time. Why not females? You are strong, independent, powerful and in control of your own raging hormones, right? Well, don't answer that. (Ha-ha!) What's worse is if you have to move in with your parents because you need the assistance so you can still work or go to school. BYE-BYE social life for 1-5 YEARS.

I read a story online where a teenage daughter (17 years old) was messing around with a bad boy in school. The mother despised him and wanted her to break up with him every day they dated. The daughter didn't out of spite for the mom. Well, six months later, the teenage girl got pregnant right before she was going to dump him (for all the right reasons). Now? It's TOO LATE! She and her parents are now stuck (i.e., connected/linked/related to) this bad boy (and his anger management + abusive behavior issues) and his parents (who aren't exactly sane/stable themselves) for LIFE!!! Grrrreat! Remember this, "A moment's bliss can turn into a lifetime of regret if you're not careful what you do or how you choose to spend your time and with whom."

A MESSAGE TO TEENAGERS & THEIR PARENTS ABOUT HAVING SEX WITH OTHER TEENS

How old are you? Under 18? Over 18? I bring this up now, up front, because if you're under 18 years old, and you're reading this book, the answer is NO – YOU SHOULDN'T BE HAVING SEX, PERIOD! Since you're a minor, underage, can't enter contracts legally, can't even rent a hotel room, have no life experience or work history to get a good paying job, can't afford a car, doesn't have a car (maybe), and a whole host of other don't-haves because you're a MINOR ... you have no business having sex. Sex is a mature/adult activity between two adults who can AFFORD any SURPRISES that might come along unexpectedly like? A PREGNANCY. Just think of someone you know (in your school) who got pregnant. Do you want that life and her responsibilities (and loss of freedoms) to slow you down (or stop) your dream pursuits of going to college, traveling during/ after high school to discover yourself, etc.? You know what your parents will say, right? "You're not going anywhere. You have to get a job. You have baby expenses to worry about now. You had your chance at having fun, and since you chose to have fun under the sheets, well, now you're going to have to take college courses online and forgo all that college fun you were going to have when you moved away from home after graduation. Besides, all that college tuition we were saving for you is now going to go towards your first year pregnancy expenses, estimated to be around $15,000."

So, what's the lesson with all this? Don't have sex (if you're underage) and don't have sex with someone you're not in love with (or willing) to marry if something (in the pregnancy department) happens. What's more sex between two people in love is far more worthwhile and deeper than ten fast flings with ten different guys.

Postponing Marriage & Motherhood Into Your 30's/40's

What's wrong with postponing marriage into your 30s or 40s? Nothing. Millions of men and women get married in their 30s and do quite well. Let's give credit where credit is due, but that's them and not you.

What I want to do for you right now is to bring up 21 key items to take in BEFORE you approach your 30s/40s. If you're in your 30s/40s, and if you read this list and agree 80% or more its truth, then you just validated what I'm saying here for the younger generation of women to listen up carefully and take heed. We're all in this together, and don't worry, there's HOPE FOR EVERYONE no matter your age if you want to find love and live happily ever after.

There's someone out there for everyone. More on that later. Right now, to the list. What should women watch out for when entering their 30s/40s and STILL SINGLE?

1. **DATING becomes more difficult in your 30s/40s.** Your looks have changed, you might be under more pressure to get married so your attitude has shifted from relaxed (I have time) to stressed (time is running out). Guys don't like to do anything under pressure unless they put that pressure on themselves to improve their game, status or success. This means, your problem is not their problem.

2. **The pool of potential men/soul mates keeps getting smaller.** Either they marry off, they're divorced or going through one, still playing the field, dating women younger than you (and don't want to give you the time of day), or they're still playing video games and lovin' it more than dealing with women and their needs.

3. **When you meet a cute guy in his 30s/40s he's often already married.** It's true. Some 25-30 year old female jumped at the chance when you didn't and snagged him as hers. "Go find your own," she says. "He's mine."

4. **Men look at women in their 30s/40s as leftovers from a decade or more of sleeping around with other men.** No way do they want to go near that snatch. Seriously. What kind of STIs or other problems have you picked up by then dating and sleeping around with too many men for too many years. Besides, if you couldn't win his heart, why not? "Hmm, I'll pass," he says.

5. **Men don't want to marry a woman with baggage, just like women don't want to marry a man who doesn't have income.** It gets very financial at this stage. If he has money, he'd rather date/marry someone who can make a fresh, clean start with him. Why would he want to pick up the tab for another guy who left you in the state you're in. (i.e., 1-5 kids, etc.) Single moms are better off dating/remarrying single dads.

6. **Some men are divorced in their 30s/40s and not ready to jump back into marriage, if at all.** So again, the pool of prospective men to marry shrinks a little more.

7. **Men view modern, independent, feminist women as women who don't need them, are competitive, combative, not feminine enough, more masculine ... and so? Bye.** They go their own way having fun with their friends, hobbies and women who don't compete against them or apply pressure to get married or have babies. They like those things to take their natural course. Date, get serious, propose, get married, have kids, grow old together. Something like that.

8. **Ask yourself, do you want to be the last single person in your group of, now married, friends?** Then, you better hurry and find your man before you are the last one in your circle of friends.

9. **Now that you're in your 30s/40s, NOW you see how having a conventional relationship and family is something you want.** While it's not too late, your pickings are getting slimmer. There's hope. I cover how to attract and choose a man at the end of this book. Keep reading and learning!

10. **Biology is real. What you think in your head about waiting or you have time or whatever is a LIE.** You've been brainwashed into believing there will always be time to find the perfect man. Sorry to break it to you, but you don't. Everyone's looking to snag someone and men are getting snatched up left and right by pretty women who want to settle down, etc. So, start listening more to your body and less to that voice in your head. Also, listen to the voice that comes from your heart. You have to be quiet though, ask a question, and listen for a voice to come from the South (your heart) not the North (your head). Your head is "full of it" and always thinking in the moment for

selfish pleasures. Your heart "needs filling," and looks out for your best interests. That's how you should navigate your life for a more positive outcome.

11. **Men/women are different. Accept it. The majority of women CANNNOT marry down in age. Men can. Accept it.** What does that mean for you at 35/45/55? You're going to have to marry someone your own age or older. Deal with it and act on it. Play your cards according to your gender and not his. Apples and oranges. Think for YOURself to survive.

12. **You may know more about what you want, but that doesn't mean you can be picky. Pickings are slimmer from 30-50 for women.** As I say later in the book, ditch the list and go for my 3 C's: COMPANY / CONVERSATION / COMPANIONSHIP. If you can give and receive those three things from/with a man, you've got yourself a winner. Anything related to what he wears or how in shape (or not) he is can be worked out together afterwards. Look for those 3 core values in addition to being responsible, has a good job/career, likes what he does, is liked by friends/family, doesn't argue, etc. I've got THAT list for you at the end.

13. **The illusion of infinite choice has now come to an end. That phrase, "someone better might be just around the corner," NEVER COMES!** Just look at your track record of 5-15 years of turning corners or waiting for someone better to come along. Let me tell you something, they don't, or they WILL WHEN you're already involved with someone. Your job in a relationship is to help improve someone to your liking while they help improve you. I don't mean to say it like "improve" you, but being in a relationship should help each other become better people. Grow together. Improve one another together. Think of a relationship like going to work for a company. Do you start out with 15 years of experience helping to make them

and you a big ol' salary? No. You come with what you've got and improve yourself and the company over time. Same thing with relationships.

14. **In your 20s, you scoffed at the idea of settling down.** Don't worry, millions do. You were having too much fun or chasing after that dream career. Now that you're older, the fun is gone, friends are married and living their own lives and you're all alone. Now what? Exactly. Keep reading.

15. **In your 30s/40s, everything becomes more segregated.** Couples hang out with couples, parents hang out with other parents, and eventually, you stop being invited to events, because why would you want to be hanging out with couples, parents, kids and babies when you're single? This is the territory you're now swimming in during your 30s/40s.

16. **Is it okay to be scared about the future? DAMN STRAIGHT, you better be!** Think about it like money/income, shouldn't you be scared if you don't plan for retirement well enough? Do you want to be poor in your 50s, 60s, 70s? If you're alone, that is a terrible spot to be in. You're not going to inherit anyone's social security or insurance policy pay out. You'll be all alone, broke or living paycheck to paycheck from Social Security. Well, as with money, the same goes for your love life. Treat your love life like your finances: #1) work hard (seek love/romance, not fun/flings), #2) save more than you spend (appreciate the good in men, don't brush them off for being nice), #3) don't waste your money (i.e., unlike money, once you waste your time away in your 20s/30s, you can't get it back), and #4) live a conservative life with a family you create.

17. **Most single people in their 20s don't see that by the time they reach their 30s/40s, they're too lazy to go out** and do all that partying and spending money on booze and late night

rides home drunk. They'd rather stay home and??? If you have a husband and kids, they become your entertainment (at home). No need to go out. Ladies, you could at least marry by your mid-late 20s, live life with your hubby, then have kids and share those experiences with your kids going into your 30s/40s.

18. **If all this sounds unromantic and terrifying, then appreciate the harsh reality of it.** When it comes to saving a life, sometimes we have to hear the bad news so you can make the correct adjustments in order to turn things around and live life on high, in love, and the way it's supposed to be lived. (i.e., NOT SINGLE FOREVER!) Again, don't compare yourself to men. Apples and oranges. You have to think for YOU and deal with the cards you've been dealt (e.g., mostly by your own dealing). Also, don't be afraid to deal with this reality. You're strong, independent, empowered, right? Call on those inner strengths and face your fears. If you don't deal with it now, it'll only get harder later. Read through my book, then my suggestions in the back on how to attract/ score a man right into your life. After that happens, your worries will go away and you'll be living life as it was meant for you … IN LOVE!

19. **Don't wait until you hit your 30s/40s to start looking. Ladies in your 20s, start looking now.** Give yourself a 3-5 year window to find a good man and marry him. Ladies, in your 30s/40s same thing, but with a different mind set, as I explain the back of the book. You'll find your man, I know you will. Despite any age, everyone has a lot to offer any relationship.

20. **What do most women in their 30s/40s think to themselves when lying in bed alone, night after night?** "I wish I would've picked someone when I was 25 and picky, but just

made it work." Well, one thing's for sure, you don't have to give up that attitude of choosing someone and "making it work!"

21. **The thing to do right now, if you're in your 30s/40s, is get a physical/check-up.** How are you physically? What does the doctor say about you being able to have children? It's good to know from any perspective. Then, double down on eating really well, removing more stress and B.S. from your life, learn to cook (if you don't or know how by now), and more. Again, I discuss in more detail what to do in the back of the book, but you get the idea. Make yourself as attractive as possible and get out there and snag your man.

Maybe by now, you don't really want to see these numbers, but I think it's important to see from this point of view. Doing so will help you keep in mind the clock on so many levels and what your options are when it comes to finding available men in certain dating pools and within certain age brackets.

WOMEN IN THEIR IN THEIR ...	20s	30s	40s	50s
% OF SINGLE AVAILABLE MEN	70%	60%	50%	40%
Married Men	10%	35%	30%	25%
Divorced Men	5%	15%	35%	45%
MGTOW Men	15%	15%	25%	35%

While these numbers might be off by 10-15% in certain demographics, they are still pretty accurate. So, what is to be learned from these figures? Well, for starters, the early bird does get the worm! So, while you have your fun, keep your eye on the clock. Don't be the last person on the bus or to snag a husband or be looked at as leftovers. Save yourself for the one for you and try snagging him sooner, rather than later. It's rough to date and find someone in your 30s/40s.

Too Career Focused
& For Too Long
(Pros & Cons)

First, let me say this, I do not want any woman to give up her passion or desire to pursue the kind of work that makes her happy or puts money in the bank to take care of herself. By all means, ladies, you go for it!

You should know, one of my biggest inspirations for why I work so hard in what I do is my MOM! After my mom divorced my dad, I watched her work several jobs, while raising two young kids (my sister and I were 5 and 6 years old in the 70s), while putting herself through night school to get her B.A. Wow, if she wasn't a driven woman, I don't know. So, I admire any women who chooses to go down that road. "All power to ya!" Let me get out of your way. I'm proud of you. You're an inspiration to us all to get off our can and work hard too! Thank you!

The trouble comes when you want to start a family. Can any

of us really DO IT ALL? We can TRY, but we're all limited to the amount of time we can really commit to doing that one thing or two or three. Even when my sister asked me to take in my nephew his senior year of high school, I didn't waste one second and asked my mom if she'd move to another state for a year just so the parenting role wasn't solely on one person's shoulders (i.e., mine). Growing up in a single parent home when I was a kid, I knew the benefit of two people parenting a child.

She willingly obliged and we took him from a 1.5 GPA to a 3.0 GPA in one year. My mom played the good cop and I happily played the bad cop, which was never needed. My nephew was a good kid. I think it was the environment I provided for him that helped him successfully shoot through the roof to a higher GPA and happy graduation experience.

That said, when it comes to a career, think of work like this:

1. **Rarely does anyone have a career. Most people have JOBS that pay enough to cover the bills.** You know what J.O.B. stands for right? It stands for Just Over Broke. Jobs come and go. We grow bored and want to leave for another one, especially if there's more money involved. Not all companies like paying their employees more just because they've been there longer or acquired more skills/know-how on the job. Again, jobs become mundane and so does going out every weekend with your friends. "Really? Can't we go somewhere different? We've been going to the same hangout for 5 years. Besides, I'm tired of spending $100 a weekend on booze and food. I'm getting fat!" Eventually, you want something beyond your job/career that is more satisfying and closer to home and your heart, which is? ... A FAMILY you can call your own.

2. **One income, as you can imagine, barely helps make**

ends meet when two really does the trick. Of course, we can thank our government and the FEDERAL RESERVE for allowing the dollar to lose so much of its purchasing power over the past 50+ years. Thanks, guys! NOT! Because the dollar buys less, you need more of it to just survive. Well, there are only so many hours in the day to earn more dollars. So? People pair up to help split expenses. (i.e., roommates, couples, etc.) Think ahead, and know if you changed/lost your job/career, you'd feel better knowing there was a second income coming into your household from your significant other to help cover most of your core expenses. His income pays for the essentials, while your income pays for any and all incidentals and/or emergency experiences that pop up from time to time because you saved your money well. Didn't you? Let's hope so.

3. **Some men wonder if career-focused women have time for a family, let alone a relationship.** We want to respect your wishes, but like many who think they can do it all, remember there's only so much time in the day. What do you want more, a career or a relationship? Now, if your career is paying big bucks, absolutely, don't chuck it quite yet. This is where a deep conversation with your future man comes into play. "Husband-to-be, you know my career pays a lot of money and I shouldn't give it up right now. (He agrees). So, what can we do to spend more time together while I keep this job, save up a lot of money for us and then perhaps transition out of the job format into working more for myself at home …" Not that you have to transition, but whatever options you have, and you know what they are, perhaps discuss them with your future man. Options, options, options. Create them, weigh them, sleep on them and then act on them.

4. **Women who tend to put off marriage and family until later, usually wind up regretting it.** Again, most women

don't have careers, they have jobs. Jobs come and go. Families you create are yours forever. Prioritize what you really want in life. What would you say to yourself, at your age now, if you were 70 or 80 years old looking back on your life? What would you do/choose differently? THEN, ACT ON THOSE WISE WORDS WITHOUT HASTE!

5. **If money is all you need, and you don't care too much about having a job/career, per se, why not take your passion/hobby/interests and start a home-based business?** With Internet eCommerce as huge as it is today, why not work from home and be with the kids? You could work part-time and still make a full-time income if you're smart about it. You also get tax write-offs for doing so, unlike that crappy W2 job/career where the government takes upwards of 40% of your paycheck. How can you live on that? Yikes! Then, when you file, they challenge you on how you filled out your tax return, causing you extra worry and stress. (Ladies, learn about FairTax.org. Just go there and start educating yourself on how our tax system is a mess from the top down and keeping 100% of what you make is what the FairTax is all about.)

6. **What you think now about your job/career potential, and it taking off a few years from now, typically turns out to be pie-in-the-sky thinking.** Thinking you'll be making more money, have more exposure to more prospects for love/marriage rarely, if ever, it happens. Ask those who've been doing what they have been in their jobs/careers for 5-10 years. If they're still single, well, you have your answer. Those better prospects never came around. If they're married, I bet 60+% of them settled for someone in the office or they met at an outing who was kind, nice, responsible, semi-good looking, made a move on them, they accepted, got to know them, took inventory of their age and

time clocks, sealed the deal and got married! They settled for "Mr. He'll Be A Good Father To MY Children" that I want to have. "I'll take him!"

7. **I don't have to go into how the #MeToo movement is putting a damper on finding love in the office.** You already know that, see that, have experienced that, right? Men don't even want to associate with women anymore for fear of being accused of sexual harassment for merely smiling at a woman or bumping into her coming around a corner too fast in the office. Ladies, you're in trouble NOW. You've got to help turn all this around. I talk about this in the upcoming *Feminism* chapter for ways and ideas on how you can help men and yourselves return to the fun state of mingling in the office like the days of old.

I could say more on the career thing, but I think you get the picture. No one wants you to give up your dreams, goals or aspirations for the kind of work or field of expertise you want to pursue if it brings you personal satisfaction to your life. Just know, it's hard to do it all. Perhaps this advice is what you'd like to hear:

1. **Get your education first and out of the way as young as possible (age 18-24).** Choose a degree (or two) in something that actually pays real money in the real world outside of college. Today's college programs offer so many bubble-headed topics for degrees. They're a real joke to companies who are ready to pay good money for men/women to do real work for them. Colleges are like any other business. They're in business to sell you something, and in their case, degree programs and debt. Remember that. There are no promises for jobs after you graduate to pay off those loans. That's your problem. They sell degrees; some hard and some easy to achieve. Choose wisely. The generic

degrees couldn't get you a job cleaning dog cages at a pet store. Don't go for those. Research "degrees that don't pay" vs. "degrees that pay" online and pursue a degree that will pay the bills and give you job satisfaction.

2. **Out of college, work your tail off to save money while having some fun.** Live at home if you can, so you can save more than you make. Getting a roommate is a good idea too, but be mindful. Living with female roommates has its problems, as you might know more than I, being a guy writing this. Living with a guy though, can have its perks. You get to live with a man (without having sex, remember), and you get access to his friends. If you like the roommate you're living with and he doesn't turn into someone you'd like to marry, what about his friends? It's an numbers game and he's got plenty of friends and his friends do, too.

3. **While working, start looking for a man to marry.** Do not give in to the temptation of giving him a lot of sex (if any) up front and do not move in with him. This will only start a multi-year cycle of come and go boyfriends. Date first, read all my books, get him to read all my books (or listen to the audio) and think seriously about finding someone by age 25-27.

4. **How's your career going by now?** Still going strong or have you switched jobs or experiencing a career change? You see, that's the thing, isn't it? Careers are for the 15-30% of people in this world who found something they can run with for a lifetime. Do know, those careers typically require a lot of study/education, commitment, etc. and usually generate hefty student loans, which demands that you stay in one place working for 20 years to pay off those loans. Not in every case, but you get my drift. That said, if jobs come and go, don't think about wasting another minute repeating this

cycle for the next 5-15 years. FIND A MAN and start a family.

5. **Did you find him? Did he propose?** If so, keep working your tail off and SAVE SAVE SAVE!!! You're going to want to quit your job and spend time with your baby at home, if you choose to (i.e., best decision for the baby and you). The man will keep working to pay the big bills, while your monies are spent on those things related to your new family.

6. **While at home now, start your own business.** Make an extra $500-$2,500 a month from home. You can. Millions of women are doing that right now. You never have to return to the job/workplace environment with crummy pay and 9-5 slave hours again. Forget about that. Jobs/careers are overrated unless you're pulling down $65,000+ a year. Yeah, that's what most women are making today. NOT! I know you are.

7. **How are we doing so far?** You're home, with child (and another on the way; congratulations) and you're home-based income is on the rise. Heck, maybe the husband can quit and work with you at home. It's happened before to millions of others. I've seen it happen with my own clientele. It can happen to you.

8. **You have your second child, your family is growing, your incomes are good, life couldn't be better. Right?** Or, what path did you go down or see yourself going down? Whatever it is, I'm sure it's right for you and in accordance with your inner drive, desires and aspirations. Just be mindful of time, job scarcity, job pay (getting lower and lower with more people looking for work while robots replace us all), man scarcity and those slim pickings and job/career burnout come your 30s/40s. No one wants to work forever; we just have to because we're not born rich. Right? You bet.

I think you get the idea again that men love it when a woman is able to make her own money. They love to see her blossom into something driven by her passions. Work makes everyone better people. Work does the soul good!

Men also don't want to have to foot the bill for EVERYTHING. That's too much pressure on them. Don't you add to that kind of pressure. Marriage is a financial agreement between man/women. Understand that. Maybe you don't see it that way, but HE does. You might see children, a home, sharing and creating memories together. There's nothing wrong with that. Just know, while relationships start out in love/romance, when/if that love goes away and you end up in divorce court. It's all about the money, honey, and that's what scares him. As mentioned, it's getting harder and harder to find quality jobs out there that pay enough to raise a family. Food, shelter, clothing, education ... it's getting more expensive to raise a family these days. So, keep these things in mind as you grow older. Find someone you can pair up with early on, share expenses and save. While you're doing that, you're probably building a family at the same time. Good for you two.

Now, if you're in your 30s/40s and you're still in love with your career and it's loving you or not, it's time to look at your finances and see if you can take some time off to spend more time looking for someone to dedicate your time to instead of the company. I'm not saying quit your job, no way. I am saying, if you don't make looking for a man a priority, he won't just show up. So, try dropping those late hours after 5:00 pm and/or working on weekends. That's what I'm talking about. TIP: If you're working in x-field, find other men in the same field who are single. Ask them out, first! DON'T WAIT! You can't wait anymore in your 30s/40s. YOU have to take action on your own in order to improve the odds of you finding someone for you. Men would come up to you in your 20s, and for the most part, you probably shot them down. Well, they're not going to approach you now. YOU may have to make the first move. That's the environment you created for men when you were younger. Maybe not you personally, but your sisters sure did. So, in your 30s/40s, it's a different ball game if you want to catch a man.

BOOKS I RECOMMEND YOU READ AFTER MINE

Home-Alone America: The Hidden Toll of Day Care, Behavioral Drugs, & Other Parent Substitutes

by Mary Eberstadt

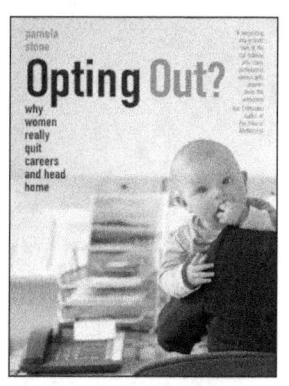

Opting Out?: Why Women Really Quit Careers and Head Home

by Pamela Stone

Day Care Deception: What the Child Care Establishment Isn't Telling Us

by Brian C. Robertson

7 Myths of Working Mothers: Why Children & (Most) Careers Just Don't Mix

by Suzanne Venker

Dating An Abuser & Not Leaving Him ... NOW!

I don't have to spend too much time on this subject because this one is very clear to me. Ready? IF the man you're with, whether you're dating him, want to date him, engaged to him, or standing at the altar and wondering if you should RUN FOR YOUR LIFE. Maybe you should versus getting too deep in a marriage with a abuser/loser. I only have these words for you ... GET OUT! Run for your life. You deserve better.

How do you get away? You stage it. You plan it. You set up your entire environment so that one day, you just DISAPPEAR. Then, having gotten the help from other positive/helpful males in your life (i.e., father, uncle, brother, friend, etc.), you use them as a shield for 1-3 months to help ward off the abuser's anger for you leaving him. No worries though. Guys will put other guys in their place quickly, let alone be your bodyguard as you move things out of his house or whatever your situation is. GET HELP. PLAN IT. THEN ACT ON YOUR PLAN TO ESCAPE.

If you stick around an abuser and continually take his abuse, then you need to look inward to see if you have your own psychological issues that need addressing. Seek help immediately from parents, siblings, family members, loved ones, counselors, etc. Get their perspective as to what you should do then act on it with laser focus. Put your blinders on and focus on the finish line of getting away from him.

You see, LIFE IS TO BE ENJOYED. I have a rule I mention inside my book, **Laws Of The Bedroom**, which his, "Men, your #1 job is to make her laugh 100+ times a day. You do that, I don't think she has a reason to cry on your watch or live in fear that you'll ever raise your hand against her. You're too busy making her happy." What's more, when it comes to arguing, always, sit down and talk together on the couch or in a calm setting. Agree that you will come to a conclusion after you both listen to each other completely, then weigh all the options on paper or do all the research. You want to come to mutual harmonious conclusions every time. That's the rule. It's not about who's right or wrong, it's about how does the final answer serve you both.

Ladies, you need to think not just for yourselves, but your children. Moms around the world divorced their husbands for fear of him taking out his rage on the kids. Yikes! Again, I don't need to say anything more about this topic than, ladies …

YOU DESERVE PEACE, LOVE & ROMANCE 24/7

That's all. Go where you can get that and leave when you don't. No negotiations, no questions, no nothing. LEAVE. He can talk to the hand.

P.S. Another note I'd like to mention from one of my other books, **B.S. The Book**, where I say, "You're not paid to be his therapist." That's right. If he has issues, you are not there to fix them. You don't have the time or the expertise, most likely. So? Leave. Find someone who will treat you better. PERIOD. END OF STORY … *MOVE ON!*

BOOKS I RECOMMEND YOU READ AFTER MINE

Losers, Users & Abusers & The Women Who Love Them: How To Break Free From Destructive Relationships & Get The Love You Want

by Michelle Hollomon, MA, LMHC

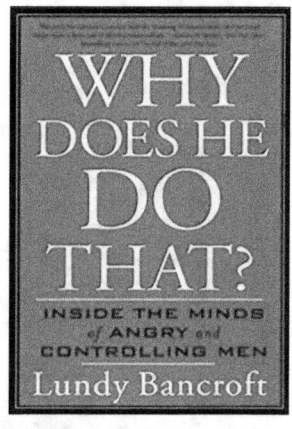

Why Does He Do That?: Inside the Minds Of Angry & Controlling Men

by Lundy Bancroft

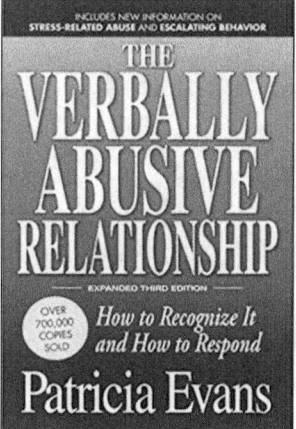

The Verbally Abusive Relationship: How to Recognize It & Respond

by Patricia Evans

How He Gets Into Her Head: The Mind Of The Male Intimate Abuser

by Don Hennessy

Personal Habits, Traits & Behaviors (That Can Drive Him Away)

This is a biggy and a touchy subject all in one. So, let's get to it. Ladies, I hate to say it, and you know it's true, but you can be your own worst enemy sometimes when it comes to keeping a man in your life or pushing him out. Many women have a bad habit of being self-saboteurs, just as men do too. They sabotage their own relationship by exhibiting any of the following personal habits, traits, behaviors, or even brainwashed mind sets. Can you relate? Has anyone ever told you that you could be annoying in some way?

From an outsider's point of view, that is, being a man, I can see women for who they are in how they treat men because I'm in the direction of their attention, interest or a lack of, in how they treat me, whether I'm a total stranger, friend, business associate, colleague, potential boyfriend/husband material, etc. Men also confide in me about how women treat them at different stages of their lives (i.e., age, money/income-wise, etc.). Men (and women) write about it all over the Web. Nothing is made up anymore. It's out in the open, well-documented and experienced by MILLIONS of men out there. What I've tried to do here is to summarize what's going on out there where women are concerned and what drives men away from them so you, too, can see it, learn from it and hopefully act in a way that keeps that man in your life, forever.

While I could say, "Don't take this chapter too personally," I really do mean that. Don't. Instead, remove yourself from the list for a moment as if you've never done any of these things. Read it over from top to bottom with a subjective point of view and hear these men out, authentically. Then, turn to your female friends, sisters, mothers and any other women in your life and ask yourself, "Have you seen them do these things to men? Have you seen women be harsh to men, exhibit these traits and behaviors that cause the men in their lives to go away? Did those men try to give their all only to wind up feeling it wasn't enough and left?"

So, without further adieux, ladies, here's what men don't like about the women they encounter, want to strike up a conversation with, ask out on a date, go out with, marry, live with and bear your children. What can you do after reading over this list to not repeat what you're about to read so you keep your man in your life until death do you part? Don't forget to share this book and this list with all the females in your life. It's important that every woman come to the table first to show her desire to mend the wounds between men and women so we can all live happily ever after.

WHAT MEN DON'T FIND
ATTRACTIVE ABOUT WOMEN

Before I get into the list, be aware that a lot of women don't like these traits about women either? So, it's just not men alone on this. So, don't diss on men for calling out these traits. Women also despise them too. In a nutshell, here's what men don't find attractive about women is ...

- **ENTITLEMENT MENTALITY.** This has to be the biggest characteristic men don't like about women. You think you're entitled to what because you're ... a woman? What do you bring to the table to feel you're entitled to ... what? No one owes anyone anything, not even drinks, dates and dinner. All things are earned. Again, what makes you feel entitled?

- **Women who let their weight go.** I blame the American diet for most of this. Whereas, in other countries, women tend to be thinner and healthier based, largely, on what they eat. Think about the Asian diet, for example, and tailor your diet to healthier choices. Enough said.

- **It's harder to approach women in America, because they get hit on all the time and assume every guy wants to get in her pants.** Well, yes, but much later. Truth is, many guys just want to talk to girls because talking with guys gets boring after awhile. So, ladies, if we approach you, be kind and give us a chance to get to know you.

- **Women are not as feminine as women in other countries.** In American, women tend to be more competitive and masculine as they got older. Just look at the movies, today, where women are punching men, kicking them around, beating them up ... "Uh, that's not the kind, sweet gal I want to date. Maybe I'd train with her in the gym, but yikes!"

- **Women in American have been trained to be spoiled, unappreciative, narcissistic and mean-spirited.** Again, where did that sweet, kind female go? Women constantly ask, "Where have all the good men gone?" Men ask, "Where have all the sweet, feminine, and interesting women gone?"

- **80% of men are tired of women only going after the top 20% of men on the social and income ladder of success.** The "I can do better" mind set is amplified with American women. Men can also say the same, "I can do better." But, you know what? Men know you're going to lose your looks in 5 years and don't care. Men really just want someone they can spend time with; enjoy life with; start/raise a family; enjoy good times and meals together. 80% of women don't look like models, yet men want to go after women in this range. Do the same when looking for a guy.

- **Rage, anger, spite, bitchiness, etc.** As the saying goes, "Hell has no fury than a woman scorned." Ladies, you've got to learn to relax, breathe deeply, take things slowly, the world will come to you if you let it. When you think of men and women, think of the waves (women) crashing on the beach and those rocks (men) stopping the waves from consuming the people there. The waves are beautiful to watch. Look how high they go. Wow, that was a real crasher. Then, the rocks/boulders/cliffs just stay there, solid as rock and calming the waves down. Ladies, take on a few traits from the rock. Men, don't be so boring. Take on a few traits from the waves. Together, men and women will live harmoniously ever after.

- **Stop blaming men and take some responsibility for your own life, actions and decisions.** Men are responsible for everything they do, good/bad. They get called on their sh** all the time. Women, on the other hand, sometimes seem to get a pass and are never held to the same standards as men when it comes to taking responsibility for their own decisions, life choices, etc. For example, how can it be a man's fault if a woman chooses to go her own way, pursues her own dreams and then runs into life's obstacles that everyone runs into? Nobody's giving handouts to men when they need help.

- **Women can choose to work or not, and yet still complain about one or the other if they don't think their situation**

is exactly the way it should be. Men don't have that choice. They have to work, period. End of story. NO complaining.

- **In the age of equality, men must forge ahead, protect the family, put a roof over their heads and provide.** If women crave equality, are they willing to do that for a man if he makes less than her? If men don't complain about being the provider, why should women? We are *equal*, right?

- **All men want is a little appreciation for working all day, a little love and understanding, some physical attention every now and then, a sweet/kind gesture from time to time, and he is good to go day after day.** What he gets in return are demands for his time, money and energies on top of what he does for her already. More and more and more, all he sees are demands of him. She's never satisfied, never content, and in return he asks, "What do you bring to the table besides ____? And, you don't cook either. So, um, I'm going to have to think this one through to see if this is a good deal for me or not. I think I might choose to opt out of this relationship. Sorry …"

- **Like women, men need time to recharge, regroup, release, and unwind from their hard-worked days.** Do women let them have their own time, space, clubs, etc.? Think Boy Scouts here. Why is it that every woman has to go where the men are and interrupt their private time to do what men like to do alone with men? Can't you leave us dudes alone for 1-3 hours a week? This is where women are starting to want to spend more time in men's "man caves!" Watch when men/women get married how his hobbies are no longer allowed and pushed aside for family matters? The man has nowhere to go now except the garage if there's even room in there. Does she let him hang with his friends when he wants/needs to? Men are fine with you ladies doing whatever you want and for as long as you want (please, go away for awhile); just so long as you don't spend all our money at the mall or shopping online. Go and do. Have fun. Call if you need a ride or there's an emergency. In return, men only ask for a little time and space away from the world (you included) to renew ourselves so we can go at it another week at work and more, which by the way is dedicated to you and supporting your dreams of having a family and living in the kind of house you want, with all things in it the way you want. YOU YOU YOU YOU. I just need time for ME ME ME every once in awhile. Thanks, for understanding that.

- **Women who complicate things more than they should drive men batty and out the door.** Men go out of their way to avoid complicated issues whenever possible. When they do encounter them, they find a solution through logic and reason, quickly and swiftly. Men are more straightforward in that sense. Ladies, if there's a problem, come to us (men) so we can work out a solution together, quickly and swiftly.

- **Women are just as abusive to men as well.** Physically, yes, men just don't call the police, they leave or block the incoming punch to his face or body. That's called self-defense. Read the book, *12 Things They Don't Want You To Know About Domestic Violence* to learn why women too can be extremely abusive physically, to her man, even children. Verbally abusive? You bet. After a woman rapes a man's character, he'll typically walk away with his heart dragging on the floor stepped on by her. It happened to a friend of mine when his sister ran all over his heart one night in a drunken state. He said nothing while she just nailed him to the cross with about 100 nails in the form of her words. It was nasty. When she had nothing more to say, he quietly asked to leave the room and walked out of her life forever.

Women seem to think they can tread on men like ants and they're supposed to come back for more abuse? Uh, no. Just because you're insane, doesn't mean the guy is. His only word to you will be, *"BYE!"* Men have feelings too, ladies, remember that, or you'll be left ... *ALONE!*

- **Women can be quite vengeful if they don't get their way.** For example, a man and a woman start dating at work. She likes that he's higher up in the company and wants to gain ground herself. Later, he discovers she has some personality traits he doesn't want to deal with so he breaks off their dating relationship, but maintains a professional relationship at work. She doesn't see it that way. She lost her ticket to moving up the ladder without working for it like he did. So, what does she do? She tries to frame him or set him up to look bad or submit false accusations about sexual harassment with the HR department. Lucky for him he saw all this coming. He took all the right precautions to capture her plotting such falsehoods. After evaluating the evidence, she was fired and he was promoted. Ladies, play fair wherever you are/go. Justice will always be served, and the guilty, well, they go to jail or get kicked to the curb to be ... *ALONE!*

- **Women can be extremely bitter and resentful during/ after divorce in ways that scare men to pieces.** "Take him to the cleaners, girl," says one of her girlfriends. You know, if you tear a man down for all he's got and leave him with nothing, what does that say about the next man you want to date/marry? If all men were warned about what you did to your last guy, I don't think many men would give you a second chance at love. Better enjoy the kids, cat and/or dog, because no man will want to get near you if you have that kind of streak running through you. Relationship aggression, using the kids to get back at the guy with parental alienation, making false accusations, you name it. Ladies, please, for all of us, watch out and don't be like this.

These are just a few of the traits, behaviors, mindsets and characteristics that drive men away from women. What have you observed in your own life? What have you seen womens do that drive men crazy and away from them? Make note and don't do those things either. Take what you read here and double up on the kindness, being sweet, patient, not so demanding, more giving, more feminine ... anything that turns you in to the sweet, loving gal he can't stand ... TO BE AWAY FROM!

BOOKS I RECOMMEND YOU READ AFTER MINE

It's Not Him, It's You: The Truth You May Not Want, But Need To Hear

by Christie Hartman, Ph.D.

Dating Deal Breakers That Drive Men Away: 12 Relationship Killers That Ruin Your Long-Term Potential With High-Quality Men

by Bruce Bryans

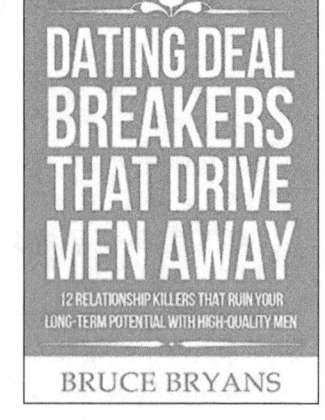

Are You Scaring Him Away?: The Top 4 Reasons Why Men Lose Interest Quickly

by Brian Nox

21 Traps You Need to Avoid in Dating & Relationships

by Brian Nox

The IRRESISTIBLE Woman: 8 Most Desirable Traits High Class Men Secretly Look For In Their Dream Girl

by Eric Monroe

To Date a Man, You Must Understand a Man: The Keys to Catch a Great Guy (Relationship & Dating Advice ...

by Gregg Michaelsen

Having Higher Income/Education Requirements Of Men

While this might seem like an easy topic to tackle, the problem is, women are setting themselves up for relationship failure and they don't even know it when they put excessive demands on men to attain when the majority can't or don't want to and yet, these same nice guys go unsnatched by these highly educated and accomplished women looking for love.

Have you heard this statistic? The higher the education a woman attains, the less likely she is to find love, a man, get married and have children? Yikes! Search online for this for proof.

EDUCATION: More men are dropping out of college because of politically correct bullsh** and anti-male hostility. They can't stand it. Not to mention all the left-wing propaganda going on making men feel guilty about being alive, no wonder college has become so pro-woman and anti-male.

Women love it because it's all about them; they're the victims, go Feminist slogans, man-bashing/man-hating professors, etc. Men are sick of it and opting out. They'd rather train to be a plumber or truck driver and make $60-80/hour than sit through some bullsh* class hearing how everything is their fault.

Where does that leave men and women? It leaves women in college pursuing all the degrees they want with funding provided by men (and women) through taxes, and men on the street to find their own way (with no help at all), whether it is online classes, trade schools, Internet occupations, various jobs that offer advancement, or starting their own businesses, etc. Women get educated/brainwashed, while men get experience in the real world of hard knocks that contradicts everything college teaches. College life is a bubble protecting you from the real world. Remember that, always.

INCOME: Occupations are changing in today's society very quickly. If we're not all careful, we're all going to be replaced by robots. Go read the book, **The End Of Work** and be fearful. Watch videos on YouTube about A.I. (Artificial Intelligence) and how robots are moving in on all our jobs.

That said, no longer do we have the kind of manufacturing jobs we used that mostly employed men. Whole industries that once were mostly employed by men are going to other countries to the way side. The industries that are booming, for example, health/medical and caring for the elderly are not jobs men gravitate to so readily. If they have to do it, they would to feed their families. Unfortunately, if you look at the pay scale in those jobs, they don't pay enough to support a family today. You still need two breadwinners.

On another note, if women are making more than men, why do

they need a man who makes more than they do? Is it selfish thinking that says, "I can have all my income to lavish me with all the things I desire and still have all his wealth to live on to pay my bills and still pursue the life I want with a new man. All my girlfriends will be so jealous." Yeah, if that isn't poisonous thinking I don't know what is. Bye, lady! I'll take this not-so-rich Latina from Brazil I met last night. She doesn't have much money, but she sure is sweet and kind to me. I give her what I can and she gives me a smile every day with coffee and the morning paper. Then, she goes off to work and, well, I'm a happy man. We have two kids and we're still in love."

Ladies, if you make more than the guy, here's what you do ... Help him start a business from home with you. Invest in the start-up and kick start him out the door selling and making money. Invest in home-study programs that teach him how to manage/invest your money to make more money. You can't do it all. You're earning it, let him multiply it. Do everything together. Nothing gets bought/sold without you knowing what's going on. Turn him into a financial wiz so the two of you can be together. Chances are? You're going to quit your job some day, then what? All that money you made would be earning interest/dividends somewhere so the two of you could retire early and travel the world or whatever.

There are so few (nice) guys making the kind of money you want him to make (i.e., more than you). You have to know, those men work 60-80 hours a week to make that kind of money. How many hours do you work? Exactly. So, be careful what you ask for. More money often times means less time at home to enjoy that rich husband you married. Plus, men who make money like that can be very controlling and ill tempered to some degree. Not all, but some. How will you find out unless you marry him? Then, you're stuck if he's the wrong type.

Better to find a really nice guy who makes more/less than you, and invest your time (even money) in him (like he would you) so you both get to KEEP EACH OTHER and grow your income higher together over time. Get this, 90% of women marry into wealth; 10% of men marry into wealth. What's that say about men not caring if you have money or not? They love you with or without and just want to be with you. Why can't you show the same level of appreciation, EQUALITY, and warmth and see a future together rather than needing him to make more money? Suppose he does for six months after you're married, but loses his job? What if you lose yours and he makes a lot of money? Would you be okay if he left you because you lost your high-income paying job? Do you see the hypocrisy?

I think I've said enough for you to realize that money, income and salaries, let alone education, don't guarantee happiness in a relationship. It's extremely materialistic, a falsehood and cannot be relied on to maintain a healthy relationship from start to finish.

Before we head to the next section, I'd like to share a scene with you from one of my favorite movies called *Tombstone* ('93). Kurt Russell plays Wyatt Earp, a retired sheriff looking to get rich with his brothers in Tombstone, AZ after retiring from law enforcement in the Midwest. Dana Delany, plays Josephine Marcus, a traveling young actress exploring the Wild West on a series of her own adventures in theatre. Well, after he loses virtually everything trying to kill off the cowboys who perpetuated terror and random acts of violence, he had nothing left and was then encouraged by his good friend, Doc Holiday, played by Val Kilmer, to do the following …

Doc: "Go grab that spirited actress and make her your own. Take that beauty and run, and don't look back. Live every second. Live right up to the hilt. Live, Wyatt. Live for me." *(Doc was dying.)*

Soon after he left, Doc to die at the hospital. Wyatt chased after her and found her. Attending one of her shows, he walked into her dressing room where she's contemplating her next move and looking back, probably thinking about Wyatt. Quietly, he opens the door and from behind her says in a deep, manly voice:

Wyatt: "Have you ever see the sun come up over the Rockies? It hits all of a sudden and below there's California, and you swear you're lookin' at heaven." (Josephine, surprised, turns around to look at Wyatt with a BIG smile. Wyatt, then goes on to say ...)

"I have nothing left; nothing to give you. I have no pride, no dignity, and no money. I don't even know how we'll make a living, but I promise, I'll love you the rest of your life."

Josephine: "Don't worry, Wyatt. My family's rich. What shall we do first?"

Wyatt: "What you wanted to do the first night we met. Remember?"

Josephine: "Uh, no ..."

Wyatt: "May I have this dance?"

Josephine: "Yes."

Wyatt: "... and then we'll have room service!"

Wyatt and Josephine embarked on a series of adventures. Up or down, thin or flush, in the years they spent together, they never left each other's side. Ladies and gents, reading this book, especially this chapter on education and income requirements for one another, focus NOT so much on the *money aspect* (in the other person), but who they are as a person and their quality of character. Money is always earned, made, lost and earned back again. Focus more on finding someone you can "embark on a series of adventures" with. Up or down, thin or flush, throughout the years, find that someone whom you'll never leave their side. Promise me, you will do this, okay?

BOOKS I RECOMMEND YOU READ AFTER MINE

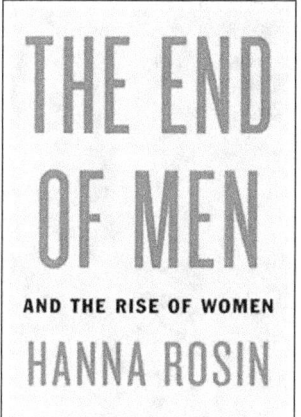

The End of Men & The Rise Of Women

by Hanna Rosin

The Decline of Men: How the American Male Is Getting Axed, Giving Up & Flipping Off His Future

by Guy Garcia

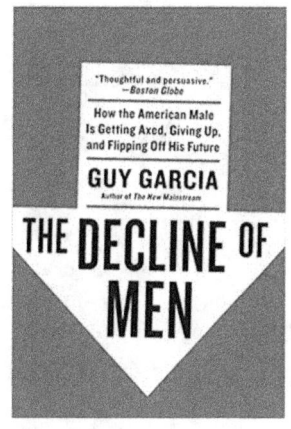

The Decline of Males: The First Look At An Unexpected New World For Men & Women

by Lionel Tiger

Mr. Perfect vs. Mr. He's Good Enough ("Yes, I Will ...")

So, you've been searching and waiting for MR. PERFECT to come along so you can snag him as yours, right? How's that going?

1. **How long have you been searching? 1-3 years? 5-10 years? 15-25 years?** How old are you now? How long have you been single? How many boyfriends (and live-in boyfriends) have you had? How many one-night stands or hook-up (kick-to the-curb episodes) can you count? Did you have any kids with men you're not married to or dating? No matter how long you have been searching, chances are you won't find him if you haven't found him by now. The older you get, the chances for finding him will keep slipping away like grains of sand through an hourglass. So, as of now, you're still SINGLE, right?

2. **Throughout the years, several (average) men *did***

approach you, but you turned them down or away for one reason or another. Maybe they turned you down, too?

3. **Your standards were, and probably are, still too high.** That list of criteria (your perfect man must meet) is and probably will forever be virtually unattainable by the average man.

4. **Do you even know what the perfect guy looks for in his perfect gal?** Do you really think you're the perfect gal for the perfect guy? Chances are you're not (perfect) or the perfect guy would have picked you out of the crowd by now. How many years have you been on the market? Don't answer that.

5. **Who IS scoring the perfect man? The perfect woman, no doubt.** Let's see if you're one of them. Do you have a "0" size figure, long legs and slim body? Are you model-like beautiful? Are you rich? What kind of car do you drive? What kind of work do you do? Are you feminine or masculine? Are you in shape or packing on an extra 15-75 pounds? Do you have a deep, hard voice or a soft, feminine voice? Are you needy, clingy or the dependent type in any way, shape or form? Do you focus on career or finding a man to start a family? Do you have time for a relationship? Can you pay your own way or must (you insist) he pays all of your way? Can you cook? Are you open to learning how? (Note: Your children don't want to eat at McDonald's every night.) I could go on, but you can see how this list is impossible to meet even by 1% of the women out there! That's how many perfect women there are for the perfect guy.

REALITY CHECK = NO ONE (GUY/GAL) IS PERFECT!

BUT, working together in a relationship, both men and women can become **PERFECT FOR EACH OTHER**. That's how I feel about it. I'd like to think you could too, and ditch the fantasy checklist of impossible standards in men you're looking for so you don't go through life ALONE anymore!

When it comes to finding the perfect man (or woman), think about it like buying a house. You've looked at 10-20 different homes in your area, not across the state/country/world (i.e., dating websites/apps). None of them were 100% perfect, and each of them had something you loved and weren't so fancy about, but you knew you could live with it or fix it (i.e., work on over time). The main thing was, you saw **"<u>POTENTIAL!</u>"**

So, what do you do? You went back home, made a wish list of all the things you would love to DO WITH that new home and then, you pictured it being the perfect home afterwards? You put time, money and effort into it. How long? Days? Weeks? Months? YEARS? How about a combination of all of those! In the first week, you bought x-supplies and made instant upgrades to some part of the house that made you really happy. Great! Next month, you're going to do y- and z- making it homier. As the months and years go by, all that time, effort, patience and investment will pay off and you will have your perfect home.

Like the home you buy, the same goes for finding the perfect man (and woman for us guys). EVERY BODY (guys/gals) listen up … NO ONE IS PERFECT. We are all as we come, in the shape we are, the state we are in, at the age we are at, physically and mentally, etc. With time, thought, care and investment, every man and woman can become the perfect man (or woman) to each other for the sake of the couple as a future unit; as ONE!

Here's a quick list of what the PERFECT GUY is for you, ladies. The perfect man you want in your life has these 10 qualities. Look for these and bypass all the rest. Those other qualities you thought were important (i.e., car, money, possessions, prestige, excitement, etc.) can be acquired within time. What you need now is a man who has these qualities:

1. **He is <u>HARD WORKING</u> and passionate about his job, career, and/or business or FINDING ONE!** No bums or video gaming couch potatoes allowed in your life, of course. What's more, he is FRUGAL and doesn't squander his/your hard-earned money on anything that doesn't have a positive return to you, himself or the family as a whole.

2. **He is a <u>FAITHFUL HUSBAND</u> (to be)** who will never forget the day he took your hand and said, "I do," at the altar. From that day forward, he is committed to making you happy for LIFE! Until that day, he *wants* to marry you.

3. **He is a <u>LOVING FATHER</u> to your children.** "Mommy, I love Daddy. He's the greatest Dad I could ever have!" He wants to have kids with you. He sees your unborn children in your eyes when you make love together. He wants to start a family.

4. **He <u>LISTENS</u> to you with all his time and attention when you're feeling sad/down.** This is very important. Is he observant? "Honey, are you okay? Wanna talk about it? C'mon, let's sit down. Tell me what's wrong. How can I help?" That's a great guy, gals!

5. **He is <u>PATIENT</u>, <u>CALM</u> and never rushes to judgment or anger.** A man who controls his own tongue and temper can help maintain harmony in the house, always.

6. **He is <u>FUNNY</u> and <u>CUTE</u> in special ways you discover in time.** A man with a good sense of humor will make you laugh when you're having the worst day ever. When you're feeling down and out, thinking back on something he said or did puts a smile on your face every time.

7. He **LOVES (AND IS LIKED BY) OTHER PEOPLE and goes out of his way to be kind to them.** His respect extends to your family and friends.

8. He **CONFIDES IN YOU before making decisions that not only affect him, but you and your family.** Making decisions together is something he loves to do because it gives him a chance to spend time with you and involve you in his life.

9. He is always **THERE FOR YOU in ways no man has ever been there for you before.** He has your back. He's there to be your rock. He's there to protect you and be that strong person to lean on. He treats you like no man has ever treated you before, either. He stands behind you, he inspires you to go after your dreams and is there to help you celebrate when you cross that finish line and every one thereafter. This man is one of a kind. He is your perfect guy!

10. **HE IS/MIGHT BE/WANTS TO BE GREAT IN BED**. I say it like that because not everyone is born to be a great lover, but if they try, learn and with practice (do help him), anyone can turn up the heat of passion and learn to ravage you like a tiger in the heat of the night a few nights per week. Heck, give him my book, *Laws Of The Bedroom*. It's the only book he'll ever have to read on this subject. Read it yourself (or with him) and act out on so many of my suggested LAWS! PASSION ... a must in any relationship.

What qualities come to your mind when you think about HOW you would like the PERFECT MAN to **#1) TREAT YOU** and **#2) MAKE YOU FEEL**? Forget about looks and what kind of car he drives or line of work he does. Cars get parked in the garage at night (can't see it) and hopefully the work stays at work, while your home remains a fun playground for relaxation and rejuvenation for the two of you and your (future) family.

At the end of the day, one of the greatest things you could ever want (and get) from the perfect man before falling asleep together are: **HUGS**, **KISSES** and **CONVERSATION** (in bed). Don't tell me, if you had those things every night you'd still be waiting around for (your imaginary) MR. PERFECT who doesn't exist? Did you know 80+% of men are capable of giving you hugs, kisses and conversation every night before bed? That means there are a lot of potential candidates out there for you to choose from. "Where did all the good men go?" They're all around you! Give them the time of day and start talking to them.

Only time, effort and energy invested in any one man will ever generate Mr. Perfect. If you agree with the TOP 10 TRAITS to look for in a guy, I bet you WON'T be single for long.

WHO IS THAT PERFECT MAN YOU CHASE, ANYWAY? THE TRUTH ... REVEALED!

THAT PERFECT MAN you chase is really nothing more than a mirage in the desert, which you will never reach. Perfect men are sought after by millions of women that can lead to ego inflation and cheating after he settles down with one of them, for the time being. He likes the adoration so much he misses it and may have a hard time giving it up. So what's the harm having a few mistresses on the side? You're all right with that, right? Uh, NOT!

Perfect men have their own set of perfect expectations of you that you may or may not be able to live up to. So, what happens? He eventually files for divorce and cheats on you during the proceedings; all because you lost your perfect luster.

Perfect men with exciting lifestyles may also have heavy responsibilities (i.e., jobs) to support those lifestyles. That means they're not at home as much as the average guy would be home for you and your family to take care of the needs that happen on a daily basis. No, the perfect man is away traveling the country/world for work, visiting his mistresses in different cities or calling escort services for fun and games behind your back. He says it's hard to come home during those 80-hour weeks, so he just talks to you on the phone and then hangs up to get back to whatever he was doing … far away from you.

As they say, the higher up the ladder (of success) they climb the farther and harder they fall. Some people don't recover after such a long fall. If you get used to a certain lifestyle and then lose it, how are you going to get it back? You risk losing friends, moving out of neighborhoods, unable to be seen at those expensive clubs you used to belong to and more. By that time you probably have kids and your figure isn't what it used to be. Finding a replacement for him might be hard to do if not impossible.

You may not know this, but any rich man probably knows how to hide/protect his assets from you should there be a divorce. I'm not talking about a prenup. I'm talking about corporations, trusts, associations, nonprofits, etc. The legal entities that can hold his money and assets without his name being attached to them means you get nothing when the divorce is final because he never owned anything to begin with. The rich know how to control wealth without owning it. That's how they stay protected.

So, marrying into wealth and then maybe one day getting a divorce thinking you're going to get some kind of big payout if the man is sharp could have prevented that before it even happened. For you to even think that way (i.e., big pay out if you initiate a divorce, which 70% of women do) means he's justified to think his way (i.e., personal asset protection) with regard to protecting what he has earned before he met you. Perfect men can also be perfect frauds. They look good on the outside, but on the inside they're rotten to the core or they're hardened, personally and/or spiritually. I've met a few very rich men in my life only to find them to be extremely boring, controlling, arrogant, no fun, etc. The average dude out there (who doesn't have that kind of wealth) knows how to have fun every weekend and wants you to join him.

If living a certain lifestyle is what you seek, maybe it's better to find a man whose *potential* can take you there. Working together on that journey, you will have really earned your right to any monies should there be a divorce. (Let's hope not, right?) What's more important is that there is a sense of humility and appreciation for the hard work you both put into creating your wealth together.

The lesson here is, don't judge a book by its cover. You want to grow old with somebody decent, kind, and loving, and before you are/look old. Change your priorities before it's too late. Save your looks (while you're young) for that ONE GUY who will commit his life to you and make you happy with your combined potential for fortune!

EXERCISE / HOMEWORK FOR YOU:

1. **The next time a nice guy walks up to you and asks if he can talk to you, let him, and TALK TO HIM!** Any guy interested in you is a good sign he'd like to #1) get to know you and #2) BE WITH YOU. Even if you're not interested initially, give him 5 minutes to chat. Be open. He's nice enough to ask to speak with you. This way, any harsh brush off you might give him doesn't turn him off from talking to other ladies he finds attractive. If all women brush off 80% of potential mates in seconds with an *"I'm not into you"*

sneer, then no man will ever feel confident to walk up to you. Learn how to say, "*No,*" gracefully, by saying "*Yes, sit down, let's chat.*" You can always call it quits after 5-10 minutes. Both of you could use the practice. Who knows, you might make a new friend. Friends have what and do what? Other *friends* and can make *recommendations!* Turn this guy you might not be interested in into a potential referral agent for you. You can do the same for him. Hey, we're all in this together. We gotta help each other. Create your own dating pool of prospects. His friends and your friends. Wow, and all that after a 5-minute conversation.

2. **Instead of focusing on his outward appearance and possessions, spend 5-15 minutes with him and find out what he looks for in the "perfect gal!"** Get him to do all the talking up front. Ask and listen to his list, then share yours. When he doesn't hear you chasing after all the bling bling, fancy cars, airplanes, trips around the world, big bank accounts, bad boy traits or hot looks, but more down home (heart-felt) qualities that he too actually wants in his life, relate to and provide you, maybe the conversation just might turn into something that generates an amazing (and not crazy and unknown) first date.

How about a phone call before that first date to continue the conversation you're having while the two of you are in your own homes? I call this SPEED DATING IN BED! Talk about the things you want in a relationship in the comfort of your own home. Role-play as if you were an item. How would it feel? Go on some imaginary ventures (non-sexual, of course). How does that feel? I bet after 2-4 hours of conversation, both of you might yield the most fantastic first date. Why? You already know so much about each other.

THE PERFECT YOU

Let's not kid ourselves. On one hand, we are already perfect with one tiny exception ... WE REALLY AREN'T. We all have our faults, fake this or that, things we want/need to work on, etc. As long as we know that and pledge to work on those things, before/during/after we find someone, hey, that's okay. What couple ISN'T still working on certain aspects of their personal lives or as a couple after they get together? Try, EVERYONE?

I can just imagine, someone saying, *"Don't look at my car. I'm so due for a new one. For now, it gets me around."* Or, *"I just joined the gym and I'm starting a 3-5 day water cleanse. I can't wait."* We're all constantly in the middle of (or starting) something to help us improve something about ourselves. Invite that someone new in your life to join you or encourage you. It's okay. What's perfect about us is our DESIRE to constantly improve, build upon and better ourselves every day of our life. THAT'S what's perfect about us and nothing else.

Another major factor in attracting someone to you is what you can do for them. Men want a woman's APPEARANCE to enhance their lives because men are visual creatures. Women want a man of ACTION to enhance her life because she thrives on survival, security and protection instincts. So? Give him/her what he/she wants. For every wish a woman wants a man to grant for her, grant one for him, ladies. Everything within reason, of course.

The best way to be sure those wishes, wants and desires get granted is to (#1) state them in the open up front, and (#2) work on them TOGETHER! *"What's gonna work? TEAMWORK!"*

You'll both get to pleasing each other much faster if you help each other reach those goals. Patience, assistance, resourcefulness, encouragement, motivation, time, attention, recognition of progress, etc. All these things play into you and him reaching your goals and granting each other's loving wishes.

KEY THINGS TO KEEP IN MIND ARE:

- **A WOMAN'S ATTRACTION** comes from her appearance and how she displays her femininity, both on the outside (i.e., dress, looks, appearance, etc.) and from the inside with her kindness, sweetness, gentleness, soft spoken tone, etc.

- **A MAN'S ATTRACTION** comes from his character of self-reliance, drive, ambition, mission/purpose, protection, and take-charge attitude, all of which could be validated by money acquired/earned, asset acquisition (i.e., home, savings, wealth), physical superiority/fitness, or having leadership qualities that can be extended to those at work and in the home.

MEN TRULY WANT TO LOVE A WOMAN

DEEP DOWN, men long to love a woman for the rest of her life, especially if they have children together. BUT, she must be careful not to drive him away and he must be careful not to be a jerk and push her away, either.

That's why guys are usually the ones asking you the question, "What do you want? How can I make you happy?" Have you ever heard a woman ask a man how can she make him happy? Ladies, suppose you asked that question and listened to his response? I'm sure his requirements are simple and easy for you to accommodate.

Don't look down on them or think low of them. They're what HE wants. If you want the car, the house, the vacations and the bank accounts, and all this "take care of me and treat me like a princess" talk, can't the man ask for something as simple as a nice warm meal cooked for him or help with his tie? He spent hours working for you to get you those things you wanted.

That's one reason why I wrote **Who's Hungry?** *(BartsCookbook.com)* so you would know exactly what a man likes to eat. I enjoy those recipes in my cookbook. If I make them for you, would you make some for me? Food brings people together. Food is a way of showing your love for someone.

Food can be sexual, sensual and help to release passion between two people right there in the kitchen. "Forget the bedroom. Jump on the counter, honey. We're gonna fool around before dinner's ready! Want to? C'mon, we've got 10 minutes. Let's have some fun!" How about learning things that make him just as happy?

But, every so often comes the vague response women give, "I don't know what I want; just not this (or that)." See the problem? If women don't know what makes them happy and if they can't articulate their needs clearly to men, then can women justify their surprise when men get fed up with trying to cater to their ever-evolving needs? Probably not.

Women keep asking for more, and while they might get it, it actually wears men out eventually to the point where they just decide to … GO THEIR OWN WAY.

Enter? M.G.T.O.W. *(Men Going Their Own Way)*

BOOKS I RECOMMEND YOU READ AFTER MINE

Get Real About Love: The Secrets To Opening Your Heart & Finding True Love

by Piane Renee

Marry Him: The Case For Settling For Mr. Good Enough

by Lori Gottlieb

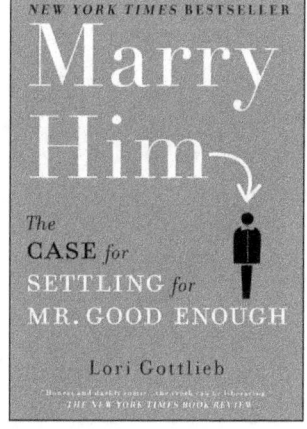

Why You're Not Married ... Yet: The Straight Talk You Need To Get The Relationship You Deserve

by Tracy McMillan

M.G.T.O.W. (Men Going Their Own Way)
– Yes, Be Worried NOW!

What is M.G.T.O.W.? What does it stand for? What impact does it have on men and women when it comes to dating, marriage, having kids, starting/raising a family, divorce, getting remarried and/or men just remaining single for the rest of their lives, hence, the phrase *"men going their own way,"* and never interacting with women ever again on any level if they can avoid it?

Well, M.G.T.O.W. is an acronym for, you guessed it, *Men Going Their Own Way*. This community of men cautions other men against entering into any kind of relationship with a women, especially marriage, because of the way men have been treated by women before, during and after marriage (i.e., divorce). For example, various institutions, such as, divorce court, the education systems, media, certain political arenas, pop culture, etc., have caused men to rethink their involvement with women based on a risk/cost/benefit analysis. That is, the cost now to get involved with a woman emotionally, financially, or both, far outweigh the benefits. So, as a result, men are choosing to … *"go their own way."*

The MGTOW community is part of what is more broadly termed the manosphere. MGTOW men have vowed to stay away from women, stop dating and not have children with women.

MGTOW men instead focus on their own self-ownership and personal pursuits in life rather than changing the status quo through activism and protests in the street, making MGTOW distinct from other men's, women's or civil rights movements that march in the streets to be heard and certain grievances resolved through legislation or by social or political means.

"WHY" DO MEN GO MGTOW?

MGTOW men use the word gynocentric to describe conditions that they claim favor women to the detriment of men, and are opposed to such circumstances. MGTOW men believe that there is a systemic gynocentric bias against men including double standards in gender roles, bias against men in family courts, lack of concern for men falsely accused of rape and lack of consequences for their accusers. M.G.T.O.W. could be regarded as a reaction to recent cultural shifts in the way men are viewed, treated and (not) appreciated in today's hyper-female culture.

Before I get into examples as to why men choose to go MGTOW, do know that **not all Western/American women are like the following women I'm about to describe**. Just know these are the qualities or traits in many American/Western women today that make it hard for men to spot the good ones from the mean ones. Like finding a needle in a haystack, finding a good woman today is just as hard as women trying to find a good man. The difference is, the majority of women (with the following traits) have turned virtually all the good men … away!

1. **Men are confused as to what women want or how to behave as a (traditional) man.** Do they open the door for her or not. Do they pull her chair out for her or not? Do they pay? Should they pay? She has her own money now. She's got the high-paying job. She's got the funds. She wants to be treated like an EQUAL to men. She's independent and strong and proclaims it everywhere she goes. "I don't need a man," attitude. So, he says, "Okay, I'm confused, sounds like you're okay ... I'll just be on my way since I'm not needed here." Hence, he opts out and goes his own way. In his own way, he's supporting her independence from men too.

2. **Men view women today as toxic, needy, brainwashed by culture/media/education,** demanding, unwilling to bring equal assets and contributions, even feminine-like kindness to the relationship table besides her assets, if you know what I mean.

3. **If a woman wants a traditional man (to pay), shouldn't he expect her to be a traditional women (and cook)?** Most women don't know how to cook, don't want to learn and find it offensive to make a sandwich for their man. Hmm, that act takes about 5-10 minutes and yet so does the act of buying her flowers. Both make each other's day and bring smiles to each other's faces. What's wrong with that? If he cooks too, why can't she? Cooking also is nature's way of saying to each other, "Let me feed you, keep you alive, make you feel good, bring smiles to our faces with these good meals, bring us together for conversation with our family after a busy day at school/work ..." Obviously, something is wrong with that, which men don't understand. So, they ... opt out and go their own way.

4. **Women drive men out of their minds and their pocket books with their "gotta keep up with Jones'" or "gotta have this and that" mentality.** For example, he wants the $30 hunter magazine for Christmas and she wants what? A $3,000 purse? Men grow tired of footing the bill all the time for her every whim only to look back on their relationship to count ... only once did she ever buy

concert tickets for the two of them. It was mostly him paying for all things entertainment related, such as dinners, drinks, dates, concerts, movies, etc. Sure, it's nice to know he can pay, but don't get mad at him if he asks you to stay in and watch a movie on TV to save a little money every now and then.

5. **Once in a relationship, or even before, women tend to move in on, diminish or limit a man's need to spend time alone and/or with his friends, to have his own space in the garage or basement for personal projects or endeavors.** Men have no problem letting a woman do whatever she feels, needs or wants to do to refresh herself, spend time with friends, give her space to be her, but when a man wants to do those things, she seems to intervene, wants to join in on, and my favorite ... "bug him" all day/night long. Do you know women like this, ladies? If you do, tell them to "back off" or he'll "back out" of the relationship sooner or later. Everyone needs space to rejuvenate from time to time. Let's give it to them before they consider going their own way.

6. **Financials and money are a big reason why men go their own way.** Having heard and read about the nightmarish horror stories of other men who've been court-raped during/after divorce, it's no wonder, they're thinking twice about entering into a relationship with a woman. Don't think dating/marriage isn't a financial contract because it is. Men pay while women consume and play with a man's money. Did you know 90% of women marry into wealth while only 10% of men marry into wealth? He sees recently divorced women looking for "sucker #2" to provide the lifestyle she once became accustomed to and wants no part of that program.

WHAT "KIND" OF MEN GO MGTOW?

- **Divorced men who have been raped financially by the courts and don't want a second woman to do the same.** They're gun shy about entering a new relationship with a woman knowing what she ultimately wants/needs from him; i.e., his money, time and devotion. Is it the same for men? Does he get her money, time and devotion. Equally? I'll let you answer that one. So, he dates lightly, if at all, or spends time with his kids on weekends if he has any. Besides that, he might be of the age where he doesn't need to be in a serious relationship anymore that leads to marriage and he's fine hanging out with friends and pursuing personal hobbies.

- **Single men tired of being rejected by women after years of trying to ask her out on a simple date** and not even once giving the chance or time of day to show he's a nice guy who wants to treat her right instead of the bad boys she's been with. So, these men go their own way. They acquire wealth and live high on life smiling all the way every day.

- **Men who were once in a good relationship with a woman. Today, they prefer to stay single due to the way women are behaving (badly) and how they behave once in the relationship.** *"No thanks. I'll live with the memories I made from being in a great relationship years ago. When women acted like women instead of today's whacked-out, bitter, demanding, whining, competitive male-like wannabe types. Thanks, but no thanks. I'll go my own way at this point in my life. Enjoy your cat/dog."*

- **MEN who have grown their finances to the point where they make a good living, maybe enough to retire early**, and don't want to have it all taken away either by the court and/or her. This means he's not going to marry you, live with you or even date you or call you his girlfriend. He's decided to ... go his own way!

Are there other types of men going their own way and choosing not to date, marry, or even talk to women? Absolutely, but you'll find them hard to track down. They're too busy living life and enjoying time with their friends (who want nothing from them besides a good time and laughs, etc.), which is what you could be doing with them if you didn't listen to what society, schools, media and feminists were cramming into your head. You know, there's a lot more to benefit from when you "think for yourself" and don't listen to what others say you should do.

THE NAYSAYERS & BLAME-GAMERS?

So, what about those who point the finger at men in the MGTOW community who wish to go their own way peacefully to live their own lives the way they see fit best for them based on their personal experiences with women or what they see out there in the dating/relationship/marriage/divorce marketplace?

It would seem, in a free country, men aren't allowed to do what they want. That is, walk away from a potential bad deal when they see it. Isn't everyone allowed to do their own thing as long as they don't bring harm to anyone? Work the kind of job they want? Live where they want? Dress how they want? Drive the kind of car they want? Eat what they want? Who gave anyone the right to rule over anyone's mind, heart and soul? This is a free country, right?

If dating and marriage demands are placed on men for the benefit of women, shouldn't there be equal demands for women to show up, participate and contribute equally in those relationship types? Or is the entire job to keep the relationship alive and intact a man's job and the woman need not do anything but show up?

These anti-MGTOW folk say MGTOW men are just as angry, bitter, sexist, or as hateful as feminists and should be viewed as such. Uh, no. Feminists want to destroy people's lives by not giving them any choice, specifically men, but women too. For example, feminists frown upon a women foregoing a career and choosing to stay at home of her own free will to take care of her children and be a loving housewife. Men don't care what women do. It's women (and feminists) who want to control what a man can and cannot do. That's all wrong. That's a dictatorship, selfish and evil.

MGTOW men are the exact opposite. To put it plainly, as they walk out the door, they're saying, "Ladies, you can have your cake and eat it too. I'm just not going to be with you." MGTOW men are also saying, "I'm not going to give you half of what I've worked for or put my heart out there for you to step on because maybe you'd like to trade up at some point in our relationship like other women have knowing it's easy for you to get some new guy and do the same thing to him. Sorry, I value my heart, my time and money too much to let that happen. See ya ..."

MGTOW men just want to be left alone to live life and pursue what makes them happy; away from feminists and female dating/marriage/divorce B.S. MGTOW men aren't into controlling anyone. In fact, that's setting women free to do what they want with your lives, too. Isn't that a good thing? Don't women want their freedom or do they really need a man in their lives?

MGTOW men have had enough with high-maintenance women, society dictates, divorce courts, legislative common law living impositions, education systems, female teachers talking down to boys, professors and ... need I continue? Remember, it's all about how we treat each other. "Treat me good and I'll stay. Treat me bad and I'll leave." Interesting, many women never leave a bad situation, such as an abusive relationship. Men, on the other hand, are quick to get out of any situation that is not conducive to his needs, health, growth or well being. Perhaps, women don't understand why men leave because THEY don't leave.

Who can blame anyone for leaving a situation that is not in his or her best interest? Ever stay at a job you didn't like? No. Ever stay in the same living situation because you didn't like it? No. Ever keep a bill or charge on your credit card because you didn't like it? No. You got rid of, got out of, asked for a credit/refund, left, went away or whatever it was to suit your needs and it was all about you. No problem. This is

America. Do as you will, just don't hurt anyone physically or get in their way of pursuing their own happiness.

Instead of trying to change females or society as a whole, MGTOW men have just decided to go their own way and let women have their lives. See the difference? MGTOW: Go your own way; live your own way. FEMINISM: Demean men, put them down, label them toxic, stay away from them, they're no good, but oh, make them stay in the relationship footing the bill for her wants, needs and desires. That's called involuntary servitude. Uh, bye!

Then, watch, any time a man stands up to speak his mind about this issue, how the media, certain women/feminists/ groups are quick to shut him down or silence or shame him and intimidate him with tactics to limit his speech. Don't believe me? The Internet and popular news and video sharing websites are known for shutting down men's voices and their (first amendment) opinions. I guess the truth hurts. Well, it's okay. The word is out, a phrase really, about men going their own way. Individually, men have been doing it and didn't even need a global community to acknowledge it. Men don't need the support of other men to do what's best for them as individuals. We just do what we want and that's it. Bye!

Telling MGTOW men they need to "grow up" or "be a man" and that what they believe "isn't real" or they're just like the feminism movement ... it's all B.S., smoke and mirrors. Men, like women, have real issues, both emotionally and financially that they have to deal with. So, they're making a decision that best fits their situation and they're going their own way with it. Rather than spending their efforts on material success to attract a girlfriend or a wife, they focus on making themselves happy. A personal decision that doesn't need the approval of society, government, or anyone at all. Internal happiness is what they want.

Men are simply responding to how they feel, how they're being mistreated by women, whether in social/dating circles, the media, at school, at work, the courts, you name it. Everywhere a man turns, he seems to run into rejection, gets his heart, mind and soul bashed and all for doing something he wanted to do for you from the beginning of time, which was to be there for you, take care of you, hold your hand, and walk with you through life 'til death do you part.

Sadly, it doesn't look like women today want those kinds of things. They want more. They want something else. They give mixed signals. They don't know what they want. Sheesh, how does a guy win besides tossing his hands up and saying, "I don't know what you want or what to do. So, bye! I'm gone."

IS MGTOW THE ANSWER?

Long term? No. Short term? YES! Every single/married woman, feminist and those who work at companies or with institutions related to anything corporate, legal, divorce courts, family law, policies, education, media, etc. needs to know and acknowledge that men are not taking any more abuse (emotionally/financially) and they're simply (and quietly) withdrawing their involvement, support and presence from anything that has to do with ... women overall and in general from top to bottom.

What's the backlash right now with the #MeToo movement? Men don't want to work with women. Heck, women don't like working for women either. Everyone prefers to work for a man. Look it up. Search, "women prefer working for a male boss ..." and read the results. It's astounding and almost as ageless as time itself. So much for women sticking together or ruling the world one day. Yeah, right.

Because of what's going on in the workplace, however, men want nothing to do with women in that arena. Companies are creating segregated workspaces or at least considering it. The result? Men get more done because they're not distracted by women. The women? Well, they're *complaining* that they can't socialize with men so they can potentially, possibly move up in the ranks or meet their future boyfriend/husband at work or at least meet them after work for a free drink during happy hour. Wow, what a mess.

Then, there's the ludicrous #MentorHer movement. If that isn't a joke, what is? Okay, so you accuse a man of sexual harassment just for looking at a woman. So, he decides not to look at her. Now, you want to encourage him to spend time with her? Who was on crack to think up that nonsense? If women know it all, are strong and independent, and don't need a man, why not get trained by a woman? It's all B.S. at the end of the day. This is how crazy it is for men out there and what they have to deal with when it comes to interacting with women.

Over time, perhaps 5-10 years from now, women will realize that good men have left to either be alone or date women from other countries/cultures that aren't as demanding, emotionally hostile, chronically insane, confused about their role in the male/female relationship and then American/Western women might come around ... *eventually!*

But, like prison, when you're removed from something you once had, like a relationship with men who took good care of you, and you now spend your days alone trying to survive and thinking about that which you don't have any more, perhaps past reflection on your own life and the decisions you made and how you treated men will sink in and cause women to rethink how you will interact with men in the future (or the present) so it truly is a WIN-WIN situation for both genders and not a WIN-LOSE (women/men) situation.

As long as men fear there's no such thing as a good woman to date in America/Western countries, they'll choose to go their own way, or like I said, look to date women from a different culture such as Asian women or of Hispanic decent. Don't believe me? Look it up online!

WHY SHOULD YOU WORRY ABOUT MGTOW?

I just mentioned why, practically. What's really bad is, eventually, the pool of potentially really good men to date/marry is going to dry up. Well, not completely, but anytime either gender loses more than 10-20% of eligible mates to pair up with, it can cause serious problems when it comes to women finding someone to date, marry, live with and have a family with.

Imagine, for example, a dating population of 1,000,000 single women and only 500,000 single men. That's a 50% difference. What's that mean for women? There are two women for every guy to choose from. If 500,000 men paired up, that would leave 500,000 women still single and alone ... for LIFE! Where are the other 500,000 men missing in action? Many have gone MGTOW or divorced or getting divorced and not ready to enter a new relationship. Some are already in a relationship, some are single and broke playing video games 24/7 at the parent's house and living in the basement, etc. Numbers like these don't work in favor of women trying to find love in this world, do they?

If more men follow their MGTOW brothers and choose not to engage in any form of relationship with women, you know where that leaves more and more women, right? UH-LONE ... for LIFE! Scary? If you're a woman reading this, you should be worried ... *NOW!*

WHAT CAN WOMEN DO TO STOP THIS TREND?

Simply put ... do the opposite of what society, the media, pop culture, educational institutions, feminists and others tell you. That's a start. Secondly, do what your heart tells you. Think with your heart and not your mind. Remember, the mind thinks short-term. The heart thinks long-term. *"That pan is hot, drop it!"* That's the mind talking to you. "He really is a good guy. You should give him a chance." That's your heart talking to you.

So, if you ever hear a second voice inside you say something like, "Hey, there's a cute guy sitting by himself. Why not go over and talk to him. It won't hurt. Could be fun." Or, "A guy just approached you. Be nice and talk to him. He may not be for you, but it's important that you not rip his heart to shreds and throw him back into the street by telling him to get lost so fast." Love works like ripples on a pond if you didn't know. What comes around goes around. If you, and every woman shoot 80% of the men down who approach you, then no man will ever approach any woman in the future except for the rough and tough bad guys who just want one thing. Besides, it's essential you work on being nice and not so judgmental or antagonistic. Work on your feminine qualities. It's a good thing.

Ladies, put yourself in his shoes when a man approaches you. If you don't like feeling rejected, think how he must feel when men get rejected far more than women do. Studies show men are twice as likely to engage in conversation with a (female) stranger when she approaches him versus when men approach a woman. The numbers drop to like 20% acceptance and 80% rejection. Well, ten ladies later, and he's been rejected 8 times out of 10. That's not nice, ladies.

Think about his feelings, like you hope he's thinking about yours. Not all men are sex-starved crazy rapists. C'mon. Most men, the vast majority of them, are kind–hearted, dedicated to making you happy and supporting you if you can be nice to him and show some feminine-like nature or qualities and not wicked, male-like competitive (or other form) of hostility towards men. That's not the real you deep down. That's you being programmed by the outside world to look down on men who only want to be nice to you and strike up a conversation. Ask him for a tip about something you need help on. Men are usually glad to help. Conversation goes a long way fast when getting to know someone. Be mindful that other women may have used and abused him to the point that they quashed every ounce of masculinity out of him. This is your chance to be nice to him and fill his tank with a few minutes of your time. It costs you nothing and it's good for your side as well. Also, encourage other women not to do those things that cause men to go MGTOW as you have just learned. Talk to them about what MGTOW means and why every woman should be afraid and play a part in bringing men back to their hearts. Are you already married? Be worried about your daughters or your sons. Share this message with them as well. I've heard mothers' concerns for their boys growing up in this crazy whacked world and not finding a good woman to date/marry. Parents with daughters should be equally concerned if they can't find a suitable young man to date/marry one day because ... *MEN WENT THEIR OWN WAY!*

TO LEAN MORE / RESOURCES

To learn more about MGTOW, check out these resources. Spend a few hours reading what's on these websites or watch a few hours of video on YouTube.com about MGTOW and learn, understand and respond accordingly so we can all fix the mess we're in. Both men and women have a role in saving our hearts and future relationships.

MGTOW.com
GoingYourOwnWay.com
EternalBachelor.com
NoMarriage.com
Twitter.com/MGTOW
YouTube.com/mgtow

RECOMMENDED BOOK

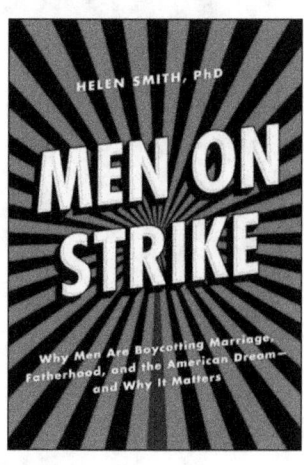

MEN ON STRIKE: Why Men Are Boycotting Marriage, Fatherhood & The American Dream & Why It Matters

by Helen Smith PhD

Porn, Fapping, PMO, Sex Bots & No More (Quality) Sex For You!

I don't know what else to say here except that porn is never good. Don't take that statement lightly. Despite today's so-called acceptance and all the hype and societal appeal, porn is damaging to your LOVE LIFE and your FUTURE with MEN! Sure, porn is stimulating, arousing, and exciting to watch, but at the end of the day, what's really going on? What are you cashing in on? Who's really winning and who's really losing when it comes to porn?

WINNING = **THE PORN INDUSTRY** and those who run these websites, financially. They win in the cash department, but not in the award department for "doing good for society." In fact, they're damaging society in greater ways than they are helping themselves. Don't let the first amendment argument fool you, either. Porn is not good for anybody, except those who make money.

LOSING = **MEN AND WOMEN** who work in porn, those who are trafficked into porn, men and women who watch porn and are addicted to porn, men and women who don't watch porn but are dating or married to someone who watches porn and is addicted to porn. I think that says it all. Did I miss anyone? So far, that's a lot of people not getting out of porn what they hoped they would. We're talking millions of men and women around the world. Instead of winning, they're losing greatly. Let's discuss.

To the point of this chapter, ladies, if you're watching porn, you need to stop. If you're dating or married to someone who is watching porn you need to get them to stop. If one of you, or both of you, is addicted to porn, you both need to stop and get help now.

Why so? Why the concern? What's wrong with watching someone get naked alone or with others for a few minutes/ hours a day, every day for years on end? What people do in their bedrooms is their business, right? Well, let's get to the heart of the matter and it's not good. Ladies, you should absolutely be terrified about the excessive use and addiction men have with Internet porn. Here's why. For starters:

- **YOU are being replaced with porn if you didn't know that already.** REPLACED and ERASED from men's minds. No dates, no sex, no weddings, no love, no nothing. Gone. Out of their minds for a long time, if not, forever.

- **You will never be able to compete with the constant influx of new naked bodies,** new kinks, bountiful breasts, round buttocks and even more female (and male) bodies flashing on your man's computer screen or his mobile device. If you think you can, you're delusional and fooling yourself.

- **You will never be able to compete with the unending search for perfection (in his mind)** and the ever-hotter sex objects appearing online every day. If you think you're hot now, start WORRYING. In a few years when your looks and beauty are going to fade. Online porn images/video never do.

- **You will never be able to compete with his growing fetishes and fantasies** to try out new things on you (and in you) and with your friends (or his) together in the same bed if he asks you one night, "Can you ask your friend to come over? I've had this fantasy about you both together doing it ..."Or, "Can I stick my __ in your __ while I __ and you __?" Or, "What do you think about swinging with other couples?"

- **You're human. You're not a computer. You're one person. You're not a blonde, brunette, redhead, black, Hispanic, white and Asian female (or male) at the same time.** Are you? Can you be? That's impossible, but that's his desire to have every night; a different woman from a different culture, for example, of which you are not.

- **You can't be edited or cropped or only show your best angles when the lights are on. Oh, he likes the lights on, while you might like them off so not to show your marks, stubble, blemishes, belly pouch, veins, stretch marks or whatever it is that makes you a real woman** and not a tanned, oiled up, lubed up, prancing around topless, bending over in a crotchless thong all day porn model ready and willing to do whatever it is without you feeling any pleasure; just him getting his rocks off ... *WITHOUT YOU!*

- **You probably aren't sexy enough for him because of all that he's been exposed to.** He's probably not aroused by (just) you anymore. He's had so much stimuli go through his hand and brain that you're just not enough. Sorry. He needs a little extra boost every time to get him going. How about porn in the bedroom while you make love, if you call that love. How about _____? Fill in the blank. Whatever you fill it in with, it's probably not healthy for the two of you, especially, YOU.

- **You could be totally naked**, walk right up to him, straddle him, put his hand on your wet cherry box and kiss him sensitively with your lips and tongue and **still be ... SECOND BEST!**

- **You can never be viewed in ten positions at once and across multiple open browser tabs**, windows or monitors at the same time. So, you're lacking there, too. Sorry.

- **You can't always be available on call when he has the urge to get off** so he resorts to porn instead of you because you allow him to (or don't know he does).

- **His computer/phone gets his love and sexual passion, thoughts and energy ... NOT YOU!** When you come home or meet him for your date, when it comes time to make love, you're ready and hungry, but he's satisfied and in recovery mode from having sex with his computer/phone. You'll have to wait until tomorrow, or a few days or maybe next week if you can catch him horny in time before he takes care of himself ... again without you.

- **Somehow, with all your passion, desire and fantasies to be with the man of your dreams and make love to him, YOU'RE JUST NOT SEXY ENOUGH.** So? He rejects you and you're left feeling you've lost your sex appeal. How's that make you feel? Really, ask yourself.

I could go on, but how do you feel about these statements so far? Can you relate to any of them? Are you afraid you could relate to any of them? Have you experienced any of these feelings before? If you can relate to what I've mentioned, or you have other experiences with porn that affect your love life in a not-so-positive way, you should be worried about what porn is doing to your love life. Get selfish here for a minute, because porn is ERASING IT! Porn erases your potential to have a healthy, normal sex life with the man you want to love. Don't believe me?

WHAT SHOULD YOU DO ABOUT PORN NOW?

What's needed is for men to step away from the computer (forever), and look at you, not pixels, not pictures or HD video with six women having an orgy together for a 25-minute sex fest or whatever his fancy is. Instead of getting his needs met with his hand, he needs to get them met through you, with you and yours too, together.

SO, IT STARTS WITH YOU TAKING A **STAND AGAINST ALL PORN**. I'm not advocating that it be outlawed or erased from our culture, but like cigarettes and drugs, we know it's there and it needs to be avoided at all costs. We know it's bad for us and we shouldn't be participating in it. If you outlaw it, then half the population would be in jail and we'd have another problem on our hands for sure.

What has to happen is WOMEN need to be made aware of the dire problem porn produces so they can help (and encourage) men to not partake in watching it.

MOTIVATION: Ladies, if you never cared about how men felt (when they got rejected by women) in <u>PUBLIC</u> when attempting to ask you out, you need to imagine how YOU WILL FEEL when you get REJECTED IN THE BEDROOM and in <u>PRIVATE</u> because you can't compete with the millions of pornographic images and videos men consume every day before they fail to make love to you. Does this thought trouble you? Have you experienced rejection in the bedroom? How about before you even go there? When was the last time you had sex with your man? Days? Weeks? Months? Years? Have you lost your man to porn? Are you about to? You could be.

If you can feel your heart breaking because this could, can, does, did happen to you, then start feeling for men and how they feel about approaching you and getting rejected just by saying, "Hello" to you. Both men and women are rejecting each other and they shouldn't. Working together, for a noble cause (i.e., love, romance and real relationships), will allow both men and women to come closer together to serve each other's needs the way nature had intended for us. You want to be LOVED, right? You want LOVE in your LIFE, right? Say, "Yes!"

Let's be real, porn is NOT love. Porn is LUST. While lust has its place in initial attraction, and at the onset of a committed relationship, it doesn't last forever and is soon replaced with real LOVE between two people spending their lives together.

Today's generation of men, and women too, are so consumed by porn that many start fapping (masturbating) as young as 10-12 years old. Girls too. Then, what happens? Boys start pushing (underage) girls to partake in sexual activities before/during/after school, when the parents aren't home, you name it. While stats show teens might not be getting pregnant as much as they used to, that doesn't mean they're not having sex earlier and more frequently, which to me, is equally troubling and bad.

For boys, by the time they turn 18, they would have been fapping (daily) for 5-6 years. Do you know what this does to a young man's ability to get it up with a real woman? He CAN'T! Never before in the history of sex have more young men experienced the highest rate of E.D. (Erectile Dysfunction) by the time they turn 25 years old. Seriously, what used to be a problem for aging men over 50, is now a problem for men under 30. Imagine that, a young man, with the prettiest young lady and he can't even get aroused by her natural birthday suit in the flesh or get it up and do what a man's gotta do. Sad and pathetic at the same time.

Now, imagine him fapping 10-15 more years into adulthood and with no real female involved in his sex life? Wow, that means YOU have no sex life. Once again, proof you are being erased from his existence. NOT GOOD, LADIES.

WHAT'S THE CURE FOR PORN ADDICTION?
★★★ NoFap & No P.M.O. ★★★

What is fapping? Fapping is a slang term for male masturbation. "Fap" is the onomatopoeia for male masturbation, whereas "schlick" is the sound for female masturbation. Yes, females are also into porn, watching it, and getting addicted to it as well.

When you hear the term "NoFap" it is meant to be a man's COMMITMENT TO ENDING HIS PORN ADDICTION AND ACHIEVING ORGASM THROUGH MASTURBATING TO PORN (PMO). Why is learning about NOFAP important to you, ladies?

- **If you've never heard of it before**, it could be something that just might **save your love life.** So, pay very close attention.

- **Porn stands in the way of #1) you finding a man who is committed to you and not his hand**, #2) you helping other women become aware of this problem to help each other understand this huge problem, and #3) you too might need help yourself to become free of porn addiction.

- **When more men choose not to date or marry because they're addicted to porn** (or porn satisfies their sexual urges and not you) then there are fewer men to date/marry! Not good, ladies.

Do women watch porn? Yes. More than ever before. Are women addicted to porn also? Yes. More than ever before. This is just not a male only addiction, even though men are affected more by porn. Sadly, folks in the media, our politicians, even our sex-ed programs in Western society all turn a blind eye to porn (addiction), it's potential harm and that's not good.

HOW DOES NOFAP IMPROVE YOUR LOVE LIFE?

There are so many ways; let's discuss them. If you know your man has a problem with porn and he does or does not know about NOFAP, then you need to talk to him. If he knows about it, but finds it hard to break from porn's stronghold, then you must help him.

You can save your relationship, your marriage, or improve the odds of getting into one with a man and keeping him attentive to your needs (sexually) if you know how to help him (and yourself, if needed) break free from porn's addictive bondage.

Quickly, here are just some of the benefits for him and you when he stops masturbating to porn, and in no special order:

- **His skin improves, his energy goes up**, his confidence returns, his social anxiety is a thing of the past and **he's horny ... FOR YOU!**

- **He becomes more attractive and physically appealing.** Men who continue to fap to porn typically don't care how they dress, smell, look, act, talk, behave, if they work or not or make anything of themselves ... please, stop him, okay?

- **Men look into yours eyes with confidence**, smiling and vibrant, alive and sincere like they never could before.

- **Under NoFap, he pays more attention to the little things about you** that you want him to notice.

- **NoFap curbs his sugar cravings, which means, he eats healthier,** which means he looks better in your eyes!

- **NoFap gives him more energy to workout**, work harder,

longer, and perform ... longer, harder ... for you!

- **NoFap can cause a man to socialize with people or friends and even strangers more confidently**. This usually yields all kinds of positive results, either in connections, money-making opportunities, fun/social opportunities, etc.

- **NoFap can cause a man to quit other bad habits** such as smoking, drinking and other addictions.

- **NoFap allows a man to focus on building the life he really wants** (hopefully with you) instead of eliminating things to make room for his porn addiction.

- **NoFap gives a man clarity of mind,** removes mental clutter and allows him to laser in on what he wants to do in life with greater precision.

- **NoFap can influence a man to dress better**, instead of the slob he might have dressed as. Ladies, how do you like that benefit?

- **Under NoFap, men don't get as upset or have negative mood swings/outbursts like they might have when they fapped.** Annoying things you once did, are now appreciated. NoFap can reduce rage and anger. Interacting with people, friends and family goes from a nuisance/interruption to a fun activity.

- **NoFap helps free him from his bedroom or private place where he holds up for hours, days, weeks, months, years at a time.** Do you miss him? Wonder where he is? What is he doing with his time, alone? Well, you can guess where he is and where his hand is too. When he's not fapping, he's outside having (real) fun and enjoying life the way it's meant to be ... WITH OTHERS and not in solitude! As C.S. Lewis once said,

"The danger is of coming to love the prison."

- **NoFap helps a man increase natural testosterone levels, a good thing for so many reasons.** For example, NoFap helps a man get back to his normal, healthy sexual energies for YOU. His rocket is harder for you and doesn't fall down like it used to when he fapped.

- **By choosing a NoFap lifestyle (commitment), men are choosing women over their computers.** By him making this choice, and with your help, he can help you feel that you ARE good enough, that it IS OKAY to be who you are, and that you can and will have a normal, healthy and naturally fulfilling sex life with the man you love. That is what you want, right?

I could go on with the benefits of NoFap, but I think you get the picture as to how important NoFap is to ridding oneself of porn addiction. I would highly encourage you to research this on your own and to learn everything you can about it. Learn what it's like to "relapse" and what men (and women) can do when that happens. Learn about terms like "rebooting" and "edging." Learn how reading other people's stories and watching videos and visiting NoFap websites can really help inspire anyone (male/female) to overcome their addiction to porn.

Why should you do these things? Because your love life depends on it. Like so many things that are harming our men (and women) today, porn is just one of those MAJOR things that is tearing apart relationships, marriages, families and preventing single men and women from getting together to start their own families. If you thought MGTOW was bad, imagine a man spending all that time alone and away from you because of porn. Now, you're REALLY not going to get him back. Well, maybe. There is a glimmer of hope.

At the end of the day, we must PUSH PORN OUT OF OUR LIVES and for good if we are to survive and achieve the kind of love-filled lives others have had and before the Internet and free porn became so readily available on our lives. Please, commit yourself to learning more about NoFap and help the men (and women) you know break free from this addiction? Here's where to go for more information and support:

TO LEAN MORE / RESOURCES

NoFap.com

BestOfNoFap.BlogSpot.com

Goo.gl/HdDtL5 *(NoFap Benefits)*

Reddit.com/r/NoFap

The-Benefits.com/nofap-benefits

Wikipedia.org/wiki/NoFap

YourGreatestVersion.com/benefits-of-nofap

WHAT ABOUT SEX BOTS & SEX BOT BROTHELS?

Okay, if you thought porn was bad, you haven't seen anything yet. I've asked people if they know what sex bots are and to my surprise, many of them don't. So, I explain what they are, which I'll do for you now. Sex robots or sexbots are "robot sex dolls" that are built to serve the sexual needs of men and women. Yes, there are sex bots made for women's pleasure, too. But, for your sake, this section is focused on men and them not giving you their attention, sexually speaking.

Now, while fully functioning sex robots don't exist YET, the technology is advancing faster than we can imagine. Know this, sex dolls are big business and manufacturers are claiming their dolls are so realistic that people are not only preferring them over real humans, they're actually MARRYING them! Seriously.

Ladies, this is very scary for you. You are about to be ERASED AGAIN from the lives of men if you don't act on what is talked about particularly in this section.

WHY SHOULD YOU BE SCARED OF SEXBOTS?

For these reasons and more:

- **Men are simple creatures that don't like a lot of small talk and communication.** If sex is on their mind and that's all they want from a woman (i.e., you know, a quick fix), well, they'll get it (sex) from a sexbot and not have to talk to her before, during or after making love to a machine. Talk about "Wham, bam, thank you, **bot!**"

- **Even though sexbots cost between $15,000 and $50,000, that's cheaper than a girlfriend, wife, ex-wife, ex-wives** over the long haul. With optional payment plans, sexbots are actually quite affordable. In fact, when they allow you to rent one for a weekend, well, it's over and you won't be invited, or maybe you will! Great, right? Uh, no.

- **Like hookers, men don't pay them (just) for the sex. They pay them to "go away" after sex.** So, like a hooker, sexbots go back into the closet after services are rendered.

If variety is the spice of life, a man could have sex with several different sexbots of different hair colors, shapes, breast/butt size, skin color and none of them would say boo about it. Just, "How would you like me tonight? Would you like your other sexbots to join us in our own menage a trois? I'm up for it if you are." I'm sure the sexbot can be programmed to say its owner's name when faking her orgasm, too. Don't forget about friends swapping sex bots.

- **Sexbots don't nag, they're not insecure, and they don't cost anything more than the unit itself.** There's no shopping for expensive items or cars or a home to maintain to keep her happy. No, the closet is fine for her after the deed is done.

- **You don't need to take a sexbot out on the town, which works great for so many men today who never could get a date to begin with** and continually get shot down for being too nice. So, he saves money and gets company at home with a beautiful sexbot of his choice, size and color!

- **If sexbots are too expensive, visiting a future sexbot brothel might not be.** Plus, you're not having sex with a real human, which means? There's virtually no guilt. Which means? The men will keep going back for more and more. Which means? No sexbot will ever get pregnant. Which means? He'll keep going back to her again and again. It will be extremely hard for any women to be able to compete with a sexbot when his sexual needs have been so fulfilled he really doesn't need you anymore.

- **Sexbots never, ever, gain weight, lose their figure, get wrinkles, grow old or show signs of grey hair.** They're always hot, always thin, always in shape, they're always naked underneath that thin piece of clothing and always ready for action even when she's just sitting next to him on the couch naked. He loves that. Are you willing to do this?

Ladies, I'm just checking in, but how are you feeling about sexbots having read what's coming next? There's no stopping this unless you help put an end to what I'm going to discuss in the next chapter on feminism or the remainder of this book, for that matter.

Granted, it's natural for us to imagine robots helping us with many things in life going into the future. Imagine every household having their own robot to cook, clean, do laundry, etc. Oh, the things women used to do and still do, but if a robot can do those things, then what does a man need a woman around for? Sex? Oh, the sexbot takes care of that, too. Company? Men are solo creatures by nature. They thrive on being alone and on their own far better than women like to be alone; especially, as they (women) get older.

Can women have a male sexbot? Sure, but they'll be more expensive and complex to build. Why? Well, a woman's needs are greater. Sexually, the position the male robot must be in is far different than a female sexbot that just lays there on her back or on her knees or leaning over on a table or in the shower, while the man does most of the work. Male robots might need to be able to carry on a conversation and listen to everything she says and then respond. I'm sure at some point, you can imagine what the male robots will be thinking about as they gain artificial intelligence, right? "WHERE'S THE ESCAPE DOOR! LET ME OUTTA HERE!" I can see those male robots running away eventually, can't you? "This is too much work, dealing with a woman, even for a robot! I'm going my own robot way!"

If you don't think this can happen, or you think companionship is something men desire like you do, then you haven't been paying attention to what's going on in Japan. There, men and women are totally losing interest in each other. What's so wrong with that trend, you might ask? Well, to put it simply, men and women aren't making babies in order to support the aging population of elderly with their taxes. Hence, the elderly become a burden to society, and the government then enacts laws allowing genocide versus health care or surgery to prolong life or live happy lives with their grandchildren ... oh ... there are none of those because men and women aren't making babies! I'm exaggerating to make my point, which I think you're grasping by now? We're (all) in trouble, ladies.

Surprisingly, you can thank feminism for pushing men faster into dating and having sex with these sex machines. Why? Well, with all the sociopathic, man-hating feminists we see every day on TV, in the news, on campuses and in the workplace, it's no surprise men are turning away from interacting with humans and prefer to substitute them for something they already love and spend countless hours with ... COMPUTERS! GAMES! FANTASY! ... and now, SEXBOTS! Heck, why not!

The constant whining and made-to-feel-guilty toxic masculinity, manspreading, mansplaining, bogus gender pay gap and false campus rape charges are all causing men to rethink, "Is interacting with women something I really want? If all I need from them is sex, then why not save up my money and buy a sexbot? It's not illegal like prostitution, and it's not immoral because I'm not taking advantage of a women. I could save up to buy a new one each year. In a couple of years, I could have 5-10 sexbots in my home satisfying my every sexual desire? Wow, my own harem! I love it. Count me in. Sign me up. I'm ready to boink my first bot!"

So, ladies, think about this, if relations between the sexes were better today, and feminism wasn't so nasty pushing men away from you, there probably wouldn't be such a demand for these fake sexbots that look and feel like a real women, right?

If you agree, then you've got your work cut out for you in helping to bring men back into the picture and into your love life the way it was meant to be. Starting with? You being nicer to men and giving them a chance. If you don't agree with that, well, then your life is your own and you are then on your own to live it … with or without … a *PET!*

Which leads me to my last comment regarding this sex-shun about porn, fapping, P.M.O., sexbots and NO MORE SEX FOR YOU world we live in! That is, if you shun men away, there will be no more sex for you. If you think a dildo will satisfy you, or your fingers will reach far down in that awkward position, which by the way removes 50% of your joy, because you're doing the work and not him, or sex with another woman and that cold plastic strap-on belt designed to reenact what a man was born with to give you every now and then appeals to you, well, you're in for a long cold winter … for years to come.

You better come to grips soon with the fact that you might not ever get any more sex again and for the rest of your life. The good news? No STD's! The bad news? No children. Oh sure, you could test-tube your way to making a baby, but I discuss that in an upcoming section. It's not the best option for you or your child (especially if it's a boy) and it is certainly NOT CHEAP.

What is cheap, and I mean low to no expense, is being kind. What is free is being honest and sincere. What is in your best interest is in rejecting feminism (not men) and the attitudes it espouses, understanding the powerful addiction porn has on men (and women) and how the behaviors and attitudes of women today are driving men away from you.

Everything "against men" should be shunned and rejected by you so you can have sex with a real man in the confines of a healthy, normal relationship, which eventually leads to . . . having children with what we all know and you want … a *HUSBAND!*

With that said, I can only imagine what's going through your mind right now. I trust you will share your opinions with me. Contact me at **WatchOutLadies.com/contact** and tell me how you're feeling so far about the book and the messages I'm sharing with you.

Having said all that I have so far in this book, I'd like to think I don't have a horse in this race, because I'm not a women, but in some ways that are important to me, even as a man, I do. Hence, why I'm writing this book. First, our country as a whole, society, for women and for men and all our futures.

Our country, our world, my friends, yours and mine, our families, the futures of, we're all in this together and to some extent, someone and/or some group, country, foreign government, socialist/Marxist ideologically-driven, unelected, behind-the-curtain organization(s) don't want us to win. You do know that, right?

Who is it? Why don't they want men and women to win together? Why don't they cherish and promote love, romance, healthy sexual relations and having lots of children? Why all the destructive and divisive attitudes? How come Feminism, for all its supposedly good intentions, doesn't promote these things? How come it's about power and independence (from men) and not happiness and fulfillment (with men). How come feminism is more about control and not choice of free will? Is feminism really a wolf in sheep's clothing?

Well, it's no secret, the stats are out. Women's happiness is at an ALL TIME LOW despite all the advances in career, income, positions up the ladder of life, job, politics, education, graduation, etc. WHY? Has feminism FAILED WOMEN? I think so. The facts of life say so. Their lack of real happiness and life fulfillment say so. Men say so. Women? Well, you just might be the last group to get on the bus to leave Feminism behind. It's not serving you like they proclaim. Let's discuss why and how you can reject Feminism to save your love life if you even have or want one to begin with. I know men do. You do too, right? Say, "Yes!" There you go!

FEMINISM B.S.
(Anti-Family Agenda, Social Fraud & Cost To Your Heart)

This chapter is going to specifically address how feminism is affecting women, men, society, children, families, and your chances at finding love in this crazy whacked out world. Of course, there have been many great advances for women from first and second wave feminism. Women can work, vote, drive, get educated, own property, own a business, get access to financial aid that men can't get, etc. I'd say that's pretty even with men. That is, apply yourself, work hard, do what you want, live life according to your own dictates and be happy. What's also amazing is that women are better than men in so many fields, such as sales, modeling, medical and health services, child care, nursing, teaching, tax preparation, advertising and promotion, public relations, ... I could go on. That's some list, eh? Way to go, ladies! *YOU ROCK!*

It's this third wave of modern, radical feminism that has everyone scratching their head wondering, "Am I really happy how things are working out between men and women with all the feminist hype, hollering and screaming at how men are so ... *toxic?*" Without men, many of the inventions we have today (designed for the comfort and protection of women) wouldn't exist. I'm not sure men are *that* disposable, do you? Men do most of the dying in wars, previously women didn't have to worry about being drafted into war. Suicide rates are highest for men, men die younger than women as they age, women inherit more money than men when their spouse dies (since men usually die off first), women typically get the majority of financial benefits when they divorce (i.e., men get the shaft); men work in some the most dangerous conditions, and, according to government research, men do most 90%+ of the dying on the job than women. So, we can talk all day long about how men are getting the shaft in life when it comes to work, sharing their monies with women, etc., but let's get to the heart of the matter, the ... **HEART!**

Feminism will say it's all about gender equality and shrinking the pay gap and everything else feminism claims to do/be for women. One thing feminism is NOT about, which, at the end of the day most women really want (besides a paycheck) and they're not getting especially as they grow older, and that's ... **LOVE!**

Feminism *(a term supposedly related to issues that matter most to women)* is not about LOVE or ROMANCE, being LOVED, finding LOVE, promoting LOVE, encouraging men to be more loving towards women, finding a really good man to date/marry, and living happily ever after ... in *LOVE*. Feminism doesn't spend one minute discussing candle light dinners, bouquets of flowers, going away on romantic getaways, bubble baths, or daily/kind gestures between men and women. Feminism will never acknowledge how much you like CUDDLING with a man or being HELD in his arms everynight. Their talk is all about independence, being strong, powerful (yeah, right) and such. How's that feeling of ISOLATION getting to you? Do you like it? Want more time (i.e., years) to be ALONE? Okay, you got it! *(I'm kidding ... keep reading!)*

IF ANYTHING, FEMINISM DRIVES MEN AWAY from you by driving a hard wedge between the genders and their hearts and desires to love one another. *"Men are the problem ... Men are to blame ... Men are toxic ... Men are rapists ..."* Wow, those sure aren't loving words to start any romance off on the right foot. When hard core, third wave feminists take this stance, guess who loses MOST? **WOMEN!**

Men are very simple and their needs are simple. If you don't need us, that's okay, *BYE!* If you choose to disrespect us and choose to beat us down verbally/emotionally/psychologically, no problem ... we walk! *BYE!*

Whenever men come into contact with any form of confrontation (mental/physical), if we can't kill it, grill it, or threaten it (with or without physical or other harm or even death to avoid such confrontation), frankly, we're outta' there. We move on. Where does that leave women when feminists try to speak on their behalf and belittle men? ALONE and on their OWN to face life and living it ... ALONE. Faced with their nastiness, hostility and wicked psychobabble aimed at men. Men have just one response ... *BYE!* ... as they walk out the door, out of your life, and go their own way ... *FOREVER!*

So, how is feminism serving you so far after what you just read? Are you happy with the outcome as to how feminists represent you and your heart? At the end of the day, are you getting what you want from men? (i.e., love, romance, time, attention, care and cuddling) Do you agree women need to be so combative, argumentative, bitter and ungrateful for all that men live for, do and die for women? You just described a feminist who doesn't get it ... ... *ENOUGH!*

When it comes to equality, feminists want equal pay, but don't want to pay for dates, drinks, dinners or entertainment with a man. Feminists only want "equality" when it benefits them. We don't see feminists pushing to get more women into higher paying jobs like plumbing, construction, trash collection/sanitation, security/soldier/policeman, oil rig workers, crime scene cleaners, truck drivers, etc. You get the idea. There was a group of millionaires who would hang out in their private club -- 90% male, 10% female. Feminists were in an uproar until they learned the men were all married and when they died, wives would inherit their millions. Fact: 90% of women marry into wealth, while only 10% of men marry into wealth. Where's the "equality" in that? Then there's the $.70 per $1.00 wage gap, which has been debunked by research and statistics. I have to say this ... 40% of a man's paycheck usually goes to pay the mortgage, with another 20% to bills, 20% for other expenses, and if there's any money left over, he saves it or spends it on his wife (or girlfriend) and the kids. What does he have left? 0%. Now, the woman makes her $.70 for every $1.00 a man makes. Let's say the man spent 10-30% of his paycheck on her in the form of gifts, good times, entertainment, drinks, dinners, bling bling, you name it. I've got her clocked in at 80-90% of his $1.00 and him down to $0-$10.00 (10% or less) left over for him. I told a woman once, during a speed dating session I participated in, when she asked, "What do you do?" I replied, "It doesn't matter, because whatever I do, I do it for you. I work to give you everything in exchange for your love, companionship, intimacy, conversation, company, our future children ..." Her reply? "I don't need to move. I found my man ..." (She was pointing to me.)

So, ladies, where money is concerned, remember, men will always make more than you because of one thing: **SEX**! All right, another reason: **COMPETITION** with other men to win your heart / cherry box (i.e., for **SEX**). All right, a third reason: **MOTIVATION**! Men are more motivated to make more money than anyone (man or woman) and to take more **RISKS,** work more **HOURS,** and **COMPETE** against other men (who are also motivated to take more risks, work more hours, etc.) so they can make more money (than the next guy), so they can win the best gal in their life! Women want security (i.e., money) and men want sex (i.e., regularly). Women do compete to attract men, but it's more about their appearance and not so much about taking dangerous risks with their life or spending countless hours on the job.

Women really do have it easy, to some extent; not always, but in some ways they do. Men don't have the same options as women, in many areas, and never will. Women can work or they don't have to if a man will provide for them. Men don't have this option. Rarely will any woman provide for a man, even though he loves her. "You don't have a job? I'm not getting near you, you bum!" Women might think they have disadvantages compared to men, men are probably making up for any of those losses in the form of working more hours, working more dangerous jobs, earning more money only to share it with the woman he dates/marries, and, in some cases, by paying with their lives. Talk about real love, real dedication, and real sacrifice. Can men be any more dedicated to women than that?

So, let's get to it ... HOW DOES FEMINISM **HURT WOMEN**, **MEN**, **FAMILIES**, **CHILDREN** and **SOCIETY** as a whole? We already know that men are constantly on the receiving end of feminism's daily (and public) hateful barrage of verbal attacks, put downs, psycho-assaults, truth bullying and other demeaning attempts to diminish and marginalize men. Wow, if that doesn't say it all there, then maybe this will:

HOW DOES FEMINISM NEGATIVELY AFFECT **WOMEN**

Feminism seems to have the awful side effect of pushing men away from women to the point that men want nothing to do with women any more, especially those who side with radical, modern, third wave man-hating feminism. Next.

HOW DOES FEMINISM NEGATIVELY AFFECT **MEN**

Read the previous paragraph. Men are going their own way, and don't want anything to do with women's hostility towards men or women who act like men. Men don't want to date/marry a woman who competes with him or challenges him. Men already get that at work. At home, they want a woman who is a woman, feminine in her nature, kind, sweet, beautiful and pleasant. This is why men are looking overseas and to other cultures that aren't brainwashed with today's feminism B.S. Done. Next.

HOW DOES FEMINISM NEGATIVELY AFFECT **FAMILIES**

For starters, few are made because men and women aren't getting together often enough, long enough or at all to start them. So, with feminism, seen by many as an attack on the family, it is the root cause of families not being formed. Thanks, a lot, feminism. NOT!

HOW DOES FEMINISM NEGATIVELY AFFECT **HAVING CHILDREN**

Because there are fewer and fewer men and women getting together to form long-term committed relationship (i.e., marriage), there are fewer children being born. With women working longer, into their 30s and 40s, still single and without a man, their chances of having children grow slimmer by the day!

HOW DOES FEMINISM NEGATIVELY AFFECT **SOCIETY**

Society as a whole, in order for it to advance and sustain its population, needs to have a minimum of 2.1 children born per family (i.e., a mother and a father). Now, if men and women aren't getting together to do the horizontal bop and have those children, then society as a whole can crumble over time. Naturally, it's also best that children be raised by their biological mothers and fathers to prevent all kinds of other problems, such as, crime, poverty, low self-esteem, discipline problems, poor academic performance and so much more. Single motherhood does not do well for children or single mothers. The stats are all over this one proving so. Now, granted, feminism is not all to blame for the lack of children being born today in developed countries, but it sure has its impact, for sure due to the large part of it plays in building that evil wedge between men and women not getting together, getting it on and having children! Now, don't just listen to me on this subject of radical, modern day feminism having its nasty effects on men and women wanting to find love and live life happily ever after. Here are a number of great books to check out to learn about feminism and why **you (ladies) should reject anything related to feminism** when it has to do with:

1. **Your HEART and not being able to find LOVE** with a man, ...

   ... *BECAUSE* ...

2. **Feminism acts so hostile towards the very men who only want to be with you, care for you, love you, die for you, have children with you, and live long happy lives with you, hand in hand 'til death do you part.** The word "feminist" needs to be discarded and feminists shunned forever if you want a real man to come into your life. **Unless women stop listening and following modern feminism ideology,** which uses fear tactics to hold you in perpetual victimhood and encourages you to continue engaging and holding onto a lifestyle that is not in your best interest, **you will most likely regret following their twisted brainwashing** when you reach your 30s/40s/50s. By then, it will cost you. No man, no family, no nuttin'.

BOOKS I RECOMMEND YOU READ AFTER MINE

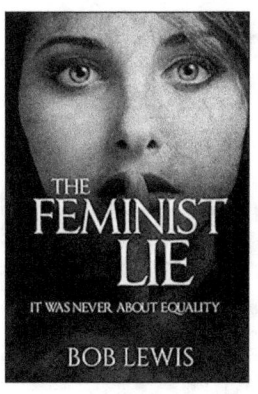

**THE FEMINIST LIE:
It Was Never
About Equality**

by Bob Lewis

**DOMESTIC
TRANQUILITY: A
BRIEF AGAINST
FEMINISM**

by F. Carolyn Graglia

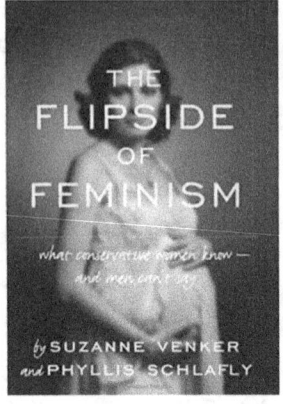

The Flipside of Feminism: What Conservative Women Know & Men Can't Say

by Suzanne Venker & Phyllis Schlafly

The Politically Incorrect Guide to Women, Sex & Feminism

by Carrie L. Lukas

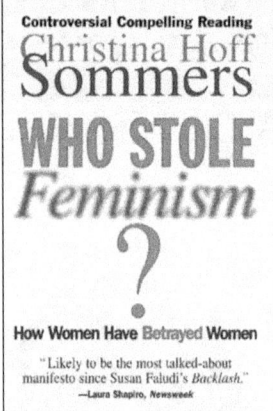

Who Stole Feminism: How Women Have Betrayed Women

by Christina Hoff Sommers

Women Who Make the World Worse & How Their Radical Feminist Assault Is Ruining Our Schools, Families, Military & Sports

by Kate O'Beirne

Feminist Fantasies
by Phyllis Schlafly

SEX MATTERS: How Modern Feminism Lost Touch With Science, Love & Common Sense
by Mona Charen

Taking Sex Differences Seriously
by Steven E. Rhoads

Who Killed The American Family?
by Phyllis Schlafly

Tilting The Playing Field: Schools, Sports, Sex & Title IX

by Jessica Gavora

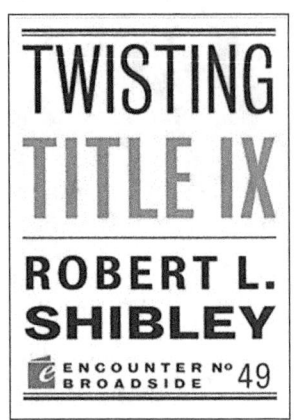

Twisting Title IX (Encounter Broadsides)

by Robert L. Shibley

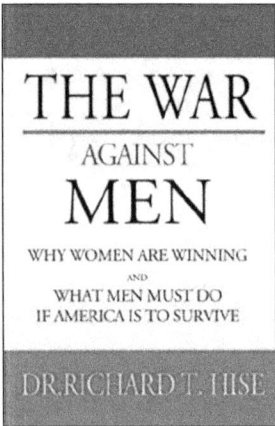

The War Against Men

by Dr. Richard T. Hise

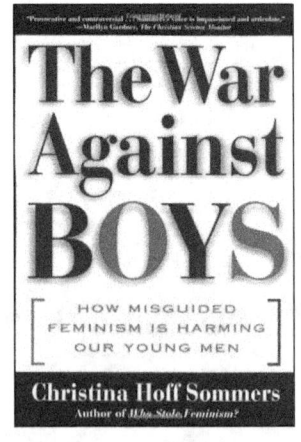

The WAR AGAINST BOYS: How Misguided Feminism Is Harming Our Young Men

by Christina Hoff Sommers

The Myth Of Male Power

by Warren FARRELL, Ph.D.

Why Men Earn More: The Startling Truth Behind The Pay Gap & What Women Can Do About It

by Warren Farrell, Ph.D.

The Manipulated Man

by Esther Vilar

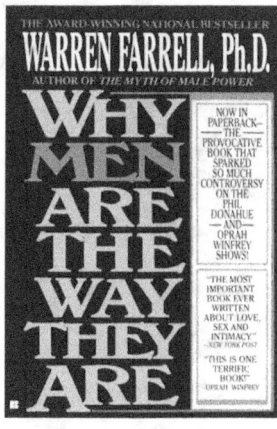

Why Men Are The Way They Are

by Warren Farrell, Ph.D.

Artificial Baby Making
& Freezing Your Eggs
(Pros/Cons/Cost)

Many women dream of having children some day, maybe after they get their college education out of the way and their careers are in high gear. Well, as the age of a woman's first pregnancy continually climbs up the ladder of time, and remaining single into her late 20s and 30s, many women are looking for ways to safeguard their fertility by freezing their eggs. Perhaps, if one day they can't find a man in time, they can dip into the freezer, pull out their eggs, make a baby and live happily ever after ... as a self-made single mom. Uh, right. Well, let's get into this and see if this is a road worth going down or not?

DISCLAIMER: I am not a doctor. I'm an author, tech designer, and a chocolate chip cookie baker. (iLoveBartsCookies.com) I do not know much about this topic well enough to pontificate because I'm not a woman either. I do not have any eggs to freeze, BUT unless this is your profession or you've done this already, many women, including myself (representing the men) are clueless. So, my aim here is to perform a little research for you to help stimulate your mind into examining the pros, cons and costs for freezing your eggs. Sound fair? You can then take this information to heart and do with it as you will. Personally, after reviewing the pros, cons and costs, it seems better to just find a man to do the deed with and start your family sooner than later. But, I know that isn't always possible. So, let's take a look at this topic and see what we've got.

AGE, CONCEPTION, YOUR EGGS & GIVING BIRTH

Age is the most important factor that affects a woman's chance to conceive and give birth to a healthy child. When women age, their fertility declines. A woman's fertility will start to decline when she reaches 30 with the decline speeding up after 35. At age 40, women only have a 5% chance of becoming pregnant in any one month. For the record, men aren't off the hook. Male fertility starts to decline after 40 when sperm quality decreases. This means it will take longer for his female partner to conceive and when she does, there is still the risk of miscarriage.

HOW DOES EGG FREEZING WORK?

In order to retrieve eggs for freezing, a woman has to undergo the same hormone injection process as in-vitro fertilization. The only difference is that following egg retrieval, they are then frozen for a longer period of time before they are thawed, fertilized and then transferred to the uterus as embryos to carry out a normal pregnancy. Once frozen, embryos can remain viable for many years with cases of live birth resulting as long as 15 years after freezing. Amazing!

HOW MUCH DOES IT COST TO FREEZE YOUR EGGS?

It can cost roughly $10,000 to harvest eggs from a woman's ovaries, but only after a woman has taken medications for several weeks to months to stimulate egg production. Then the eggs are frozen and stored at an estimated cost of $500 per year. Each time eggs are thawed, fertilized and transferred to the uterus with IVF, it can cost about $5,000. Typically, egg freezing is not covered by insurance, but paid by the women herself. So check with your carrier to see if they would cover this for you. You never know. Times change.

SIDE EFFECTS FROM IMPLANTING FROZEN EGGS

As with any medical procedure, there can be side effects associated with freezing eggs, nothing too major, but some might include nausea, mild abdominal pain, weight gain, vomiting, shortness of breath, bloating and diarrhea. It's also possible to develop a more severe form of ovarian hyperstimulation syndrome that might cause fluid to build up in your abdomen. Egg retrieval procedures have complications, but, again, nothing too serious.

WHEN IS THE BEST AGE TO FREEZE YOUR EGGS?

If you plan to freeze your eggs, and cost is not a problem, the earlier the better. Any time before the age of 35 is best. After 35, egg freezing can be linked to the same risks as getting pregnant after 35 including higher odds of miscarriage, preeclampsia, congenital abnormalities, high blood pressure and cesarean section. I'm not a woman, but I'd freeze my eggs at 20-25 years of age if I could. See if mom/dad will pay for it.

WHAT ARE THE CONS TO FREEZING YOUR EGGS?

Consider the fact that you might be 5-15 years older by the time you're ready to use your frozen eggs. You will need to consider whether your body, specifically your pelvic organs, will be healthy and strong enough to carry a pregnancy at that later age. What's more, the success of your pregnancy also depends on the health of the contributing sperm. Who is it? How old is he? 40+? Also, just because the egg-freezing technology is there and results can be promising, there isn't enough data, decades of experience, stats and results to fully understand or determine how any woman's eggs will function after being thawed. So, think about all that. I'd want to know that.

IS EGG FREEZING RIGHT FOR YOU?

It depends. What's going on in your life that you think you need to have this done? Are you busy with your career or can't find the right man soon enough so you think this might be a good option for you? It can be. Is it affordable, though? Are you undergoing some other treatment such as surgery, cancer, etc. that threatens your ability to have children in the future? There are many good reasons to freeze your eggs provided you can afford it.

QUESTIONS FOR YOUR DOCTOR

The next step, if are thinking about doing this, see your doctor and ask him/her a few questions while doing your own research online. Here are a few questions you might ask of your doctor: Am I a good candidate for egg freezing? How many eggs should I freeze? How long will the eggs remain frozen? What are the success rates you've seen? Can my eggs be negatively affected by the freezing process? What are the risks that you've seen? How much does it cost? Will my insurance cover egg freezing? Can you check? After asking questions like these, I think you'll be able to make a sound decision as to whether freezing your eggs is something for you.

SUGGESTIONS & MORE INFORMATION

I hope I've done well here to provide you with some basic information about freezing your eggs. It is exciting to even think we have this kind of technology to begin with. The flip side, as always, are the unknowns, the what-if's, etc. Just as there are concerns with freezing your eggs, the next round of concerns might be ... are you doing this alone? Are you married when you're having this procedure done? Are you dating someone? Are you single and still alone and want a child in the future?

Only you know the answers to those questions when you make the decision to freeze your eggs or thaw them out because it's time to have your baby. As I've said before, anytime a baby is born, it is a time to celebrate. That life now has a future filled with endless potential and possibility. In advance, *"Congratulations!"*

HAVING A BABY ON YOUR OWN & WITHOUT A MAN AROUND

In this last section, I only want to bring to your attention the story of someone who wanted a child, couldn't find a man to have it with, decided to have the baby on her own, and, well, here's her story and what she experienced:

1. **It was a healthy birth!** She was the mother of new baby boy.

2. **She was alone, though;** no man or family nearby to help out.

3. **She began to feel the stresses of having a child on her own** and without the extra help that typically came with having a husband to share the joys and duties of raising a child together.

4. **Some of the emotions she experienced when she was single and living alone didn't end even after the baby arrived.** She thought a baby would cure most of them. While being a mother created a new fascination with life, what was still missing was the man in her life to serve her needs as a woman and to be a father to her child. She still felt alone, scared, stressed, and with a baby now on board, her daily routine was packed with even more to do ... *ALONE!*

While I think the desire to have a baby, while single or with someone you're married to is great, I think it's important to keep in mind the realities of what it really takes to raise children on your own. My mom did it; many moms have. Is it easy? No. Rewarding? Yes. Should you wait and put more time, energy and focus into finding a suitable man to father your child? Absolutely.

INFORMATION
CONTENT
INFO
PEOPLE
NEWS
NETWORK
INTERNET
PUBLICATION
WORD
RADIO
COMMUNITIES
COMMENTS
INTERNET
SHOW
POLITICAL
INFORMATION
NEWS
VIDEO
NETWORK
MARKETING
SITE
AUDIO
VOICE
RECORD
PEOPLE
INFO
COMMENTS
ANALYSIS
GLOBAL
TV RADIO
ADVERTISING
TODAY
VIDEO
SHOW
ONLINE
POLITICAL
COMMUNITIES
INTERNET
SITE
VOICE
COMMUNITY
TV RADIO
INFORMATION
TALK
TALKING
PEOPLE
ADVERTISING
BRAND
COMMENTS
MARKETING
GLOBAL
CREATED
WORD
POLITICAL
COMMUNITY
NEWS
ONLINE
COMMUNITIES

Pop Culture & The Media (Nothing But Lies & More B.S.)

Yeah, I hate to break it to ya, but the media, pop culture, Hollywood and every glamour magazine ever   published really only has one agenda and that's to make a profit off of the slutty, uninformed, anti-family, oh, and single female. Would you agree with that assertion? Their standard protocol is to lie, fabricate, and exaggerate about anything and everything to brainwash and hook you, line and sinker, into thinking and believing that what you see (through their lens) is real and not what you were brought up to believe by your parents or what you know to be true. Would you agree?

If I told you to jump off a bridge, would you do it? Of course, not. You know that would end your life or at least seriously impair you. So, what's my advice to you regarding pop media platforms spewing lies and B.S.? Change channels, ignore them, cover your eyes and ears, look away, distract yourself, do something else, tune into things that are more in line with moving you forward with life and towards a more fulfilling life of love and not hype, lies and self-degrading behaviors that only lead to a LIFETIME OF LONELINESS. Until you do, you're just feeding out of their hands and emptying your purses with all your money. While I might be generalizing to make a point, you know most of it to be true.

The media throws up loads politically correct propaganda at us every hour of the day. We're inundated with messages on how to dress, act, behave, etc. Hollywood sets the trend. Why not? They have the budgets. We're inundated with messages 1,000 x a day. How can you escape it? Again, turn off the TV, the Internet and your phone for a while and detox from all the B.S. For example, I NEVER want you to watch the idiot box evening news at night. Let's see, murder, kill, crash, robbery, kidnapping, ... did I pretty much giveaway the news every night? You don't need that. If something (news) is that important, a friend will tell you. Let THEM be your filter. Keep your mind garbage-free. Don't go to websites looking for tabloid trash either. You don't need that in your head. It only feeds their pockets with advertiser's money.

Those who govern society, the dominant and elite, are totally interested in female empowerment and rage against men. We all know that power corrupts. Check this out, you know that those who govern society are dominant, wealthy males, right? What do they want? To liberate the whore in every woman. I think they've done it. The media, pop culture and society, in general, is pushing a completely conflicting and inconsistent message that is supposed to resonate with our hearts and keep our country heading in the right direction. Reality TV has also had its (negative) impact on how women are portrayed. I can't watch ONE SECOND of any reality housewives shows. It's not REAL! All the arguing, yelling and throwing things around in rage ... did someone forget to take their medication? Sure, it's TV, but that stuff gets broadcast throughout the world. Imagine how people in other countries view American women. YIKES! No wonder American men want women from abroad. She hasn't been corrupted by our pop culture / media B.S. like they have here in

America. Even if you agree with half of what I'm saying here, no one really gets how plugged into the Matrix we are, especially women. You don't understand that most of your beliefs come not from your own self-discovery but from powerful media and public relations type influencers who are paid big bucks to shape our world view without us even realizing it. Once you travel aboard and take notice of how other people live in other countries, you might quickly realize how screwed up our media is here and how screwed up they want us to be.

Please, ladies, take heed to what I say about the media and pop culture. Another example ... when I was growing up, the female singers of my time ... wore clothing. Today, they dress like ... strippers. Why? Does everything have to be overly sexualized? That's not how life is supposed to be. Also, ladies, social engineering is real and has been going on for decades, if not centuries. If you could understand that, even do a little research on the matter, that one simple truth would set us all free towards resisting the globalists, elitists, new world order folk and what they are trying to do to us. (i.e., put us all in the poor house, eliminate the family, brainwash and drug our kids at schools, keep the same corrupt politicians in office, keep men/women single forever, etc.) It's all done with DISTRACTION = THE MEDIA!!!!!!!

We must break free from these media-enforced ideologies and strongholds that are so deeply-rooted in our minds. The best way is to just not watch/listen to them. Done. You're free. Effective. They want us to feel incomplete and inadequate until we make a purchase and tune into their shows. THE ANSWER? Again, stop feeling the urge to buy things for that temporary rush as if you were just like some caged rat hitting a button for yet another one of their cocaine pellets. Think family or easing into a minimalist lifestyle where accumulating things is not important to you. Put your happiness on a simple budget. You're too busy creating your own life story or in search of the man of your dreams.

"The Wall" & Sexual/ Marriage Market Value (Watch Out Ladies!)

If there's anything women really need to **WATCH OUT FOR,** it's the inevitable, unavoidable, no negotiations, no escape, it will happen to you, no hiding or dodging it ... **THE WALL!**

What is The Wall? The Wall is the point in every woman's life when she is no longer highly desired by men, sexually speaking. It is called The Wall because of its effect felt by women as if their faces are hitting a wall. OUCH!

The Wall represents the point in a woman's life where her sexual market value (SMV) has fallen to a record low of near *ZERO* and her marriage market value (MMV) is flying close to that number as well. If she has kids by another man (or multiple men), this number can dip into the negatives. It's at this point men no longer find her attractive or give her any preferential treatment she once received when she was in her early/mid/late 20s.

WHEN DO WOMEN HIT THE WALL?

The Wall hits a woman between the ages of 28 and 35. Once she hits the age of 30, it *can be* downhill from there in many regards. You may have a women hit the wall sooner due to hard partying at night clubs, years of drinking, even casual smoking, doing drugs and not eating a healthy diet. All that catches up fast in the female body to the point where there is virtually no returning to the once hot body state without major diet correction and an abstinence in alcohol, smoking and drug use.

Evidence of a woman hitting the wall includes a lower sexual interest by men, a dramatic drop-off in approaches by men, fewer compliments from men and fewer invitations to converse and even hang with men. When a woman's physical attractiveness begins to fade, her SMV and MMV fade fast as well.

WHAT HAPPENS WHEN THEY HIT THE WALL?

Women, when they hit the Wall, often let their ego or SELF-ASSESSED VIEW of their own sexual market value far exceed their ACTUAL sexual market value. This gives her the illusion that she's still hot when she might not be. When women hit the Wall, some of them still feel entitled to a degree for attention they once received pre-Wall when she was at her sexual peak. This period of time can often be a very frightening time for a woman when she realizes she can no longer win interest from men with just her looks, gender and sexual offerings.

When women hit the Wall, this usually serves as a wake-up call and they realize their power over men was temporary (during their 20s) and is now fading fast along with their looks. This period usually kick-starts acts of denial along with a quick change in life priorities, such as, *"I don't have much time. My body clock is ticking. I've got to find a husband and make babies!"*

The sad part about all of this is that even after hitting the wall, some women will go on to waste a few more years testing her sexual market value on highly sought-after men and hoping to see a glimmer of light that might indicate she's still hot (when she's not). Of course, this only makes a woman feel depressed, desperate, maybe even bitter and regretful that she wasted so many years and now has to settle with someone far less than what she could have scored (in a man) when she was in her prime.

This act of "squandering her youth," for those who did, is also referred to as "riding the cock carousel" during her 20s only to wind up hearing men say, *"Time's up. The ride is over. Time to get off. Someone younger than you has come along that I'd like to spend time with and who is into marrying me. Since you said, 'No' to me during the years I wanted to marry you, I'm now saying, 'No' to you. I want to continue having fun, maybe. How's your career going? Well? Great!"* Whatever the reason, the ride is over and she now has to go home ... ALONE!

MORE BAD NEWS FOR POST-WALL WOMEN

Trends today tell us that men don't want to date or marry women over 30. Where does that leave women over 30? Alone. If the dip in her own sexual / marriage market value is depressing, what's worse is the pool of men eligible for marriage or who want to get married is dwindling to microscopic proportions every year she enters her post-wall years.

Recently divorced men don't want to get married right away or ever again if they were treated poorly by the court system or the ex-wife. Men don't want to take care of another man's baby. Men who are dating don't want/need to date another woman if they're already in a relationship, whether it leads to marriage or not. Men don't like to be pressured to marry just like women don't like being pressured for sex. While sex is a short-term activity with risk, marriage is long-term commitment with more risk to men if they lose because she could file for divorce in order to trade up as he trades in his marriage card for a jail cell for non-support. Men who are busy, doing their own thing, or going their own way don't want to date or get married. Men who were in long-term relationships are out, might be content with their past relationship memories, or want to enjoy all the perks of being single. These stats alone make it even worse for women to find men to marry after "the wall." Men also know that a woman's fertility is in decline during these years. If a man wants to start a family, naturally, the younger she is, the more fertile she is. So, post-wall, women are out of the picture.

WHY DO WOMEN WASTE THEIR YOUTH ONLY TO WIND UP SINGLE & ALONE POST-WALL?

Women, from birth are given so much in the form of protection, gifts, grants, drinks, dinners, dates, entertainment, you name it. True or not? Men get what? *"You're on your own, buddy."*

After graduation, during her 20s and during her prime SMV and MMV years, she is chasing her career and fun times, social events, free drinks, dinners, dates and entertainment. So, she thinks to herself, *"Wow, can this last forever? It's been years since I paid for anything."* This delusional mentality enables her to continue this lifestyle in excess of what she makes income-wise, if she even has a high-paying job during her 20s. Most don't. Remember, most people have jobs, not careers.

When she hits 30 and her SMV and MMV hit a sharp decline, guess what? All those subsidies, gifts, free drinks, dinners and dates are now over, gone, no more. In the meantime, what's coming into play? DEBT! She might have a student loan to pay off or maybe her credit card debt has increased over a decade of making only minimum payments. At this point, her income must be greater than her expenses to remain solvent. Career-wise, 30 is around the age where she's either growing tired of working the job she's got or promotions aren't that easy to come by any more. Why? She received a couple in the past few years. If she wants a new one, she's got to put in MORE HOURS AT WORK! Yikes, what does she start thinking about? Finding shelter. At some point in a woman's life, some eventually would like the support of a man. Not all women, but many do. Why not? Two can pay the rent much better than one, right?

We know that most men prefer younger women. If more women accepted this reality, I don't know if they'd really waste their youth on remaining single when they could catch a really great guy, settle down and start a family. Now, we all know, marriage, kids, and family isn't for everyone. All power to anyone who wants what they want. What's important to focus on here is a woman's fertility rate, youthful appearance, and sexual market value all relate to her chances for getting married.

When women ask, *"Where have all the good men gone?"* This is evidence that she has hit The Wall years. Is it fair that men openly discriminate against women who hit The Wall. Why not? Don't women judge (and decline) men on the basis of income, status and ability to provide financial support for her needs, wants and desires when starting and raising a family? Of course.

Some men believe women in their post-wall years are bad choices altogether for marriage and starting a family. Since these women spent their 20s ignoring and rejecting marriage offers from nice men, they are deemed incapable of making practical decisions, want the rich guy instead of the nice guy, unwilling to compromise or sacrifice for the good of her family ... all the must-have skills for starting and maintaining a family.

Going forward, and as you've read in the chapter on porn,

sexbots and escorts, for sexual pleasure, men seem to be better off with those options. They're cheaper, even free, and supply him with an endless array of younger women 'til his lust is content. The cost for these options is a fraction of the costs for dating/marrying a post-waller. Naturally, if one of the post-wall women were to offer sex, chances are, she's only interested in his seed and landing him for marriage or money or both.

DO MEN HAVE SEXUAL/MARRIAGE MARKET VALUE?

They do, but not to the degree women do, in the sex department, that is. If you looked at sex from an economical perspective, women hold all the cards, value and resources. Since men are too willing to have sex with almost any female, his sexual market value is lower than hers, which remains at an all-time high during her 20s (SMV years). This doesn't mean men can let their bodies go or put all their eggs in one basket (i.e., money/income). Women love good looking men, too. Remember that, guys.

Men's market value is more in the marriage department (not sex) when it comes to what he brings to the table, such as, time, attention, love, commitment, financial support, family values, father to his children, etc. Because men are valued more for what they can provide in those areas, a man could be 55 years old, a millionaire, and marry a 25-35 year old. Crazy as that sounds, it's not. *"Girls love money, like bees to honey!"* Think about the reverse. How many young men would marry a woman in her 50s or 60s just for money when he's in his 20s or 30s? NEVER! Men want sex. They're capable of making their own money when they apply themselves.

So, as a woman's sexual and marriage market value decreases as she gets older, a man's marriage market value can increase as he gets older making him a hot target for women to go after for marriage. Do men want to marry young, in their 20s and

30s? Absolutely. Men want to find that one girl they can call their own. Like women though, the media, peer pressure and other forces influence a guy's better judgement making him think about sex 24/7 and want it just the same. There is no focus any more on family, values, traditional roles, marriage, and the like from our educational institutions, the media, government, feminists, you name it. So, what do men and women find themselves doing? Having sex without commitment, single for years on end, and what else? ALONE time after time.

WHAT CAN WOMEN DO TO AVOID POST-WALL ABANDONMENT FROM MEN & INCREASE MMV?

Let's get to it. Enough negative talk. Let's look at the positive side here. Women don't need to hear any more about the realities of getting older. They need SOLUTIONS and not more observations. How can women overturn or break through the wall (back to the other side) and increase their odds for landing a man for marriage, love and romance? Plain and simple, women must focus on these areas, just as men do too to some degree. Men aren't off the hook either where these areas are concerned. Feel good about that, ladies. Okay, here we go ...

DIET (EAT LESS, EAT RIGHT, WEIGH LESS & LOOK YOUR BEST!)

It's no secret. What you eat (or don't eat) is how you look, weigh and live. A healthy diet also contributes to healthy baby-making bodies! The less you eat, the less you weigh. The better choices you make about what you eat, the better your skin and body look/function. Need inspiration? Guidance? Look at Asian women. What do they eat? They eat a lot of vegetables, fruit, rice, fish, chicken and in small quantities. Bread is out. Red meat is out. Alcohol, only in small servings and only 1-2 x per week if that. Food is our medicine for living longer, healthier lives. It's also the secret to maintaining a youthful complexion.

It goes without saying, smoking is out. Drugs, no way. Dairy? Out. Eat light, eat right, weigh less, look great and you're 25 all over again! I personally know Asian women who are in their 40s who look as if they are in their 20s or younger. Take a tip from them about eating. I do and I'm a guy!

SKIN CARE, PERSONAL CARE & EXERCISE (HELP A LOT)

While guys don't know what skin care products help to reduce wrinkles, lines and desert like surfaces on the skin, women should. Research this, ask your friends, go online and dig up the best (and affordable) skin care products to help keep your face, neck, hands and hair looking youthful. Guys can do the same thing. I do. I take care of my hair, skin and such with carefully chosen selection of shampoos and conditioners, hair care vitamins, skin moisturizers and the like. Whatever effort you put into these areas, double it! This also goes for EXERCISE. Working out is one of the best (and free) means of looking younger. I know men who don't work out whose bodies look old. I work out 4-5 x a week, sometimes 2-3 x per day. I make sure I sweat, which helps rid the puffiness in your face and neck. The more you work out, the less you eat, and the higher quality of food you consume ... it all adds up to a hot body, once again!

ATTITUDE (STAY FEMININE, NOT BITTER/ANGRY/DESPERATE)

This is a biggy with guys. No guy likes a woman who's negative, depressing, complaining, gripes, is bossy, pushy, ungrateful, self-absorbed, etc. I'm sure you could add to the list. Remember, keep it simple. What am I talking about? Be #1) nice, #2) thoughtful, #3) caring and #4) sweet. Done. You've just eliminated all the other traits many women today have in their post-wall years that absolutely push men away. The 1-4 traits I just described make you the perfect mother, wife, girlfriend, life mate, soul mate, you name it. Focus. Practice. Work on you to attract the kind of man you want in your life.

BE CONCERNED, CARE ABOUT & WORRY (FOR ... MEN)

As you've read so far in *Watch Out Ladies*, men are not doing so well, on many fronts. Their character, manhood, incomes, boyhood and desires for marrying a woman are in constant battle with today's feminist and man-demeaning media that is determined to put men down in the commercials we see, in movies, and on TV. Is it no wonder guys feel safer and are happier going their own way? Please, do not join in on the sabotaging of the male gender. Otherwise, to do so only decreases your chances of him looking at you. Remember who your competition is and it's fierce: younger women, porn, escorts, sexbots, hookers, foreign women ... need I go on? So, again, please show more care for men these days. They want you just as badly as you need them, and I did say "need." Don't put stock in the phrase, *"Women need a man like a fish needs a bicycle."* That is such a lie. How about this one then, "Men need a woman like they need a headache or a wallet-drainer?" Now that's true. Seriously, men don't need women. They WANT women. They DESIRE them and women do need men at some point in their lives. Don't think so? Try to imagine life without a man in it. Take a look at your current situation and be honest.

FEAR (SCARE YOUNG WOMEN INTO MARRYING SOONER)

Now, I'm exaggerating here to make a point, even though what I said has a lot of truth to it. A female friend of mine, who'll be 50 next month and still single, told me, *"I wish someone would have taken me aside when I was in my 20s and told me that when I was 50 I would still be single and living alone with no man. I would have made different decisions about my life and how I lived it during my 20s."* Ladies, you have more going for you at your age (30-60) than you think. Even post-wall, you can influence the relationship market in your favor. Here's how. #1) Share this book with 10+ younger women. Specifically, women between the ages of 18-28. Find them and instill the fear of God in them (i.e., pain, fear and loneliness millions of women feel at your age and whatever else you're feeling). Encourage them to consider settling down sooner than later. Literally, help them!

Now, of course, people are entitled to live their lives and stay single forever if they want. I'm not talking about getting people to go against their choices. What I care about, and you do too, is that **FEELING** of *REGRET*! The feeling alone can weigh heavy on the heart for a lifetime if you don't *watch out*!

When you scare (i.e., help) younger women with their futures for living alone, pairing up with men and stay paired up, who's left on the market? Men more your age who couldn't find a younger women, because they're OFF the market. They now have no choice but to live a single life or pair up with you. To SOME degree, this can work if all women understood that time isn't on their side (or men's either). We've all been fed a lie and need to take action to help redirect the direction our country is going in or else all future generations are double-f****d up than you think we are now. We're all crabs in that pot of boiling water.

OPEN MINDED (TO MARRYING MEN NOT ON YOUR LIST)

Remember the criteria you had for the perfect man? Tall, rich, handsome, etc.? Well, DITCH THE LIST. I think you know the quality of man you really need in your life. I described him in the **Mr. Perfect vs. Mr. He's Good Enough** chapter. Looks fade for both men and women; time to start thinking about your heart, conversation and companionship. Who can you have (clean) fun with minus alcohol, club hopping, etc. Who will be there to enjoy life with? No more struggling alone, single. Don't be against marrying a man without wealth, either. Help him start a business or become an investor from home. BAM. Done, he's now making money and you're both in love. YAY!

BOOKS I RECOMMEND YOU READ AFTER MINE

The "Rethink Remedy" For Single Women Over 30: Detox For The Marriage-Obsessed Mindset (Volume 1)

by Lori Shea

The Not-So-Patiently Waiting Handbook

by Day Dream Alston

Online Dating For Women Over 40: The Hopeful Woman's 10 Step Guide To Enjoyment & Success

by Christie Jordan

Attract Love At Any Age: The Ultimate Dating Guide For Single Women After 40 Simple Steps To Navigate Today's Dating World & Find Love Again

by Marlene Wagner

**Find a Husband After 35:
(Using What I Learned at
Harvard Business School)**

by Lori Gottlieb

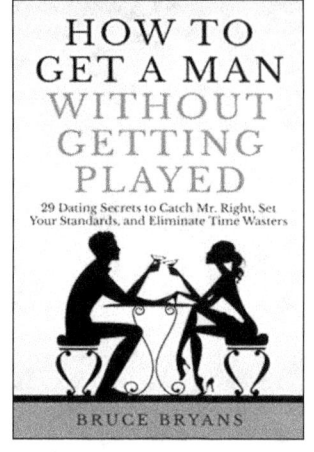

**How To Get A Man Without Getting
Played: 29 Dating Secrets to Catch
Mr. Right, Set Your Standards
& Eliminate Time Wasters**

by Bruce Bryans

Lord, Prepare Me To Be A Godly Wife

by Tiffany Langford

**God Where Is My Boaz: A Woman's
Guide To Understanding What's
Hindering Her From Receiving
The Love & Man She Deserves**

by Lori Gottlieb

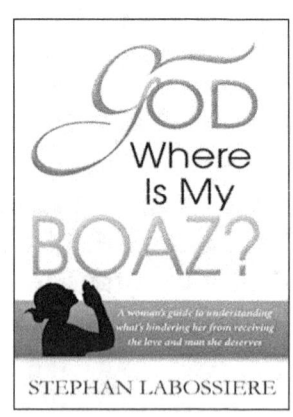

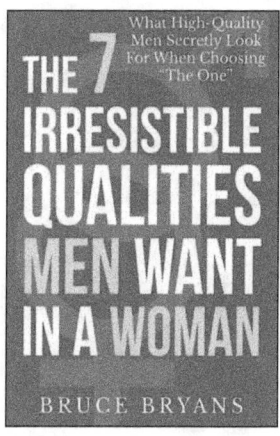

The 7 Irresistible Qualities Men Want In A Woman: What High-Quality Men Secretly Look For When Choosing The One

by Bruce Bryans

When God Makes You Wait
by Adam Houge

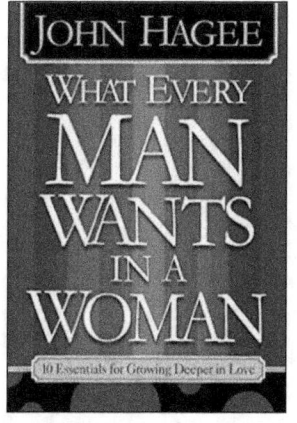

What Every Man Wants In A Woman

by John & Diana Hagee

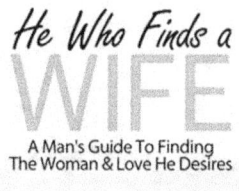

HE WHO FINDS A WIFE: A Man's Guide To Finding The Woman & Love He Desires

by Stephan Labossiere

Make Him BEG For Your Attention: 75 Communication Secrets For Captivating Men To Get The Love & Commitment You Deserve

by Bruce Bryans

Japanese Women Don't Get Old or Fat: Secrets of My Mother's Tokyo Kitchen

by Naomi Moriyama

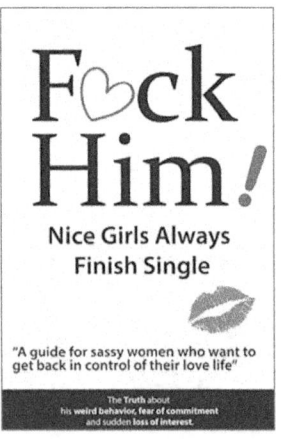

F*ck Him! Nice Girls Always Finish Single

by Brian Keephimattacted and Brian Nox

Why Latinas Get the Guy: What Men Really Think About The Choice Between American & Latin-American Women

by Joe Bovino

101 Things Your Dad Never Told You About Men: The Good, Bad, & Ugly Things Men Want & Think About Women & Relationships

by Bruce Bryans

Send Him A Signal: 61 Secrets For Indicating Interest And Attracting The Attention Of Higher Quality Men

by Bruce Bryans

Why Men Like Asian Women: Dating An Asian Woman & Why I Married Her: For Thinkers & Thickheads

by JJ Jackson

NOTHING WORSE THAN CHASING MEN! SAY NO MORE: Understand Past Love Lessons, Heal Thyself & 8 Ways To Get Ready For More

by T.R. Ruby

CONCLUSION

I can only hope that **Watch Out Ladies** has given you the kind of insight, reflection and self-observation needed from an outsider looking in so you can perhaps make the kinds of changes needed to ensure your present and future are filled with "intelligent hope" when looking for real love and romance in this crazy world while ending the single's streak you may be on right now with a string of bad guys you've been dating, but don't care to marry.

Going forward, here's my advice to you. Follow every one of the following suggestions below and I can assure you, you'll find the one for you sooner than later, or not, if you don't:

1. **Get with your girlfriends. Go over this book and read every chapter. Each of you pick something from the book and read it out loud and then have a discussion about it.** Be honest, transparent and try to find something you know you can improve on or confirm, "I'm doing that ..." Do the suggestions make sense to you? Do they resonate? Can any

of your friends in the group share a story or comment on something in particular from *Watch Out Ladies*? Make note of these lessons learned/shared and don't (or do) repeat them.

2. **Meet with a group of guys, either alone or with some of your girlfriends, and ask them to provide commentary on what you've read in *Watch Out Ladies*.** Trust me, they'll love the opportunity to vent, share, agree and maybe even ask you out because *Watch Out Ladies* brought you all together for a really good time. Involving men in this group setting will give you insight into what men are also experiencing. This might really motivate you to keep their concerns and worries in mind since you heard them speak out loud about them, personally.

3. **Be nice(r) to every man you come in contact with. That's an order! No skipping this one, please.** Exhibit lady-like gestures and thank men when they do chivalrous things for you.

4. **Initiate the first step and talk to guys. C'mon, you're a strong woman, aren't you? Once you initiate, you can let him chase you, sure.** Just keep in mind, "speed to market" mentality! If you want a man, approach him first. Remember, more men are on their way OUT the door (going their own way) because of women's attitudes and treatment. So, you better chase them down or at least ask them to stay awhile, have a drink, some conversation, etc. You might go so far as to buy HIM a drink. Remember the ripple effect on the pond I spoke about earlier in the book? When you initiate kindness, and other women do, too, men all around start sensing it, they start feeling it, and respond positively and approach you more when THEY know it's safe. One last comment about why it's important for you to initiate ... it takes the pain and suffering out of you responding to all the 100s of inquiries you might get on your dating profile. Reach out to a few you like and let them be the very few that receive your attention.

5. **Scare women younger than you so you can date men within your own age range!** (i.e., 5-10 years older/younger) Transfer your fears to them. *"You don't want to end up like me, do you? Single? At ___ years old? Then, (1) read this book and (2) find a man and settle down."* The fear tactic should motivate them into dating men more seriously and not dumping them so fast for the next higher-up guy, which does what? Magically, it takes younger men and younger women OFF THE MARKET. What's left? Older men finding (only) women their own age, single and available. See how that works!

6. **It goes without saying, after reading a book like this, hopefully you'll stop having sex with men who don't show any commitment to you,** who can't be patient enough to sleep with you, who don't find other things about you interesting to talk about, do, spend time with, etc. **SEX IS A REWARD** for **COMMITMENT**, **NOT A FREEBIE** to be given out just because you let your guard(s) down or you want to feel needed, appreciated, wanted or are on the rebound from a previous relationship. Besides, sex is BETTER in a COMMITTED relationship, anyway.

7. **Work on yourself to improve yourself. Tell no one. No one has to know. Let their outwardly comments serve as positive affirmation and reinforcement** that you're looking better and more sexy every day! If you have my other book, *Find The One For Me*, read over the PREPARE FOR THE ONE section. Model healthy eating and skin care habits from Asian women. Eat light, lots of vegetables, fish or chicken and stay away from snacks, dairy and red meat. Remember, *"An ounce on the lips is a pound on the hips."* So true, and it applies to men too, so you're not alone regarding this rule. Limit sweets and snacks to once a month or once a week, and only a few bites and not a bowl.

8. **Again, do anything and everything to help improve your looks, skin tone, body, physique, you name it.** Looking great isn't just "to catch his eye," but to make you feel great about yourself. Men love confident (not competitive) women. Even I want to look my best so I try to work out 5 days per week and sometimes 2-3 x per day. Make working out, losing weight, skin care and personal care, not only a top priority in your life, but make it a LIFESTYLE so it becomes automatic.

9. **WORK ON BEING MORE FEMININE, CARING AND NICE rather than competitive, masculine, argumentative, combative, angry, arrogant, bitter, toxic, demanding, picky, bratty, spoiled, mouthy, selfish, needy for attention, ugly (on the inside), fat, morally disturbing, entitlement-minded, self-absorbed, self-indulged, game-playing, resentful, ungrateful, manipulative, negative, speak nasty, rarely/ ever listen, power-hungry without any accountability, want rights without responsibility, think men are slaves to support you, and demeaning to others (both men and other women) ... welcome to the world of men and what we think of (most) women.** Instead, be positive, uplifting, and put smiles on people's faces by putting one on your own 24/7/365. Be everything a woman should be according to NATURE and not SOCIETY! Society only wants to profit off of you by controlling you. Nature's rules were here before you and I were born and will be here after we're gone. So, you might as well conform to what's in your best interest if you want to be HAPPY and in LOVE with someone, soon. Otherwise, keep playing your cards the way you have been and see what "tricks" you keep getting. Don't be the woman with only dollar signs in her eyes and no soul. Focus on the advantages of charm and femininity instead of constant competition and comparing yourself to men. Too many women are losing their femininity with the Feminist movement. It's so unattractive and counterproductive to what your heart really wants.

10. **Make a list of 10+ major attributes, assets, talents, skills-sets, etc., that you bring to the table besides your gender and sex appeal that men can logically appreciate, justify and feel confident to take a chance with you.** Relationships are a two-way street and giving comes before receiving. What do you bring to the table besides your company in bed. North American women, for example, expect males to be giving all the time without ever getting or asking anything back. A strong and evolving relationship requires a joint effort from both men and women. One idea is to start by showing men this book. Tell him you've read it and that you agree with 99.999999999% of what's inside and you want him to know you're going to try not do the things that would (1) drive him away, (2) make him feel you would ever leave him for reasons described in the book that make men afraid to date/marry women, i.e., divorce courts, alimony/jail, financial rape, toxic feminine behavior, etc.

11. **Study what turns men off, make a real list, and don't do (or repeat) them or you'll push men away.** You might take note of what other women do that drive men crazy and away.

12. **Educate yourself more on these topics: (1) MGTOW; (2) third-wave, modern/radical Feminism that destroys relationships between men and women; as well as, (3) porn addiction** among men and women, NoFap, and sexbots. All these topics have adversely impacted women who are trying to find love and long-lasting companionship.

13. **Commit to reading (or listening to the audio version) of 10+ books** I recommend you read after *Watch Out Ladies*. You can also visit similar websites that discuss such topics. Watch videos on YouTube. View posts on Pinterest or Instagram. Search for other venues to learn more about these important topics.

14. **Assess YOURSELF! What do you need to work on? Be honest and proactive with this. Take your time and make a list. When something comes to you, write it down.** When you have 10 or more things, prioritize them and get to work on them. Ask your friends, *"Hey, if there was one thing I could work on to improve myself, what comes to mind?"*

15. **Go back to any recent guy who expressed an interest in you and give him another shot.** *"Hey, are you free for lunch this week? I want to talk to you about something."* Then, when you meet up with him, you can say, *"Remember when you were coming on to me (or wanting to spend more time with me, etc.), well, I'd like that. We can _____ for our first date. BUT, it's just a date. You'll be on your best behavior and so will I, maybe!"* If anything, you might learn something about yourself by going out on that date. You don't have to marry him, sheesh! Going through the motions can be extremely helpful for you, your heart, and for him. You might be surprised. After a few role-playing dates, something might actually come out of it that you actually like, such as a ... *BOYFRIEND!*

16. **If you expect him to be a traditional guy and pick up the tab when you go out to eat, offer to cook him a home cooked meal by the third or fourth date. Show him you're a traditional woman and can feed the (potential) children you hope to have one day with (a) man.** Don't let him spend hundreds or thousands of dollars on you only to find out you can only make toast or boil water. Refer to my cookbook, **WHO'S HUNGRY?** (BartsCookbook.com) for quick and easy meals to make that are sooooo good and that he'll enjoy. I should know, I'm a guy, and I wrote that cookbook with my favorite meals in mind! Men don't want your wealth, they want your love and support. IF you have wealth, why not share it. Men do. Again, let's size you up? Are you a traditional woman? Can you cook? Do you want

a family? If your man makes enough money, are you willing to stay home and raise the kids? It's best for THEM. Break free from today's brainwashing!

17. **Dress like a woman and not a man, which means dresses (any length) and heels.** Save the pants for when you're alone or with your friends. Men love to see women in a dress. You look more ladylike in a dress and it will remind you that you are a beautiful woman worthy of all that glamorous attention.

18. **The next time you participate in yoga or meditation class, think of yourself as a mother (to be) and not a club-crawler, free drink-guzzling hooker, not that you are, but you get the idea.** When women have children, their perspective on life changes. It's no longer about them, but about their kids, their family and about something outside themselves that is more gratifying than another night out with the girls. When you live more for what you brought into this world than yourself, you overcome temptations and the act of wasting yet another night living it up 'til 3:00 A.M. only to find your soul starts calling for you to be something more and do something more with your life that just work and party.

19. **Adjust your view about "women's rights" (if needed) and come to grips that feminism can and does destroy marriage, family, and society.** Only a few women can wave their fists in the air, hit the streets and march for more freebies, handouts and special privileges. The majority of women MUST be homemakers and raise babies in order to sustain a stable, growing society. Who else is going to do that? Government day care programs? Run from those! We've reached a point in history where feminism will be the reason for our collapse. This is because globalists have orchestrated feminism and the economy by brainwashing us all into thinking we don't have enough and that we need more. The elitists, who planned all

this, did this to eliminate the middle class and turn everyone into a pauper. This was before advanced technology occurred when they needed a lot of slaves to make their trillions of dollars per second. As technology advances, they need fewer humans around. So, they want to extinguish a huge percentage of the human race. Sadly, many modern women don't think about that, or even care, and won't voluntarily relinquish their "rights," so they will grow old ... ALONE. Why? Because they don't fit the traditional mold of making good wives and mothers. They're too self-absorbed, too driven to support themselves and chase that career oasis in the desert of their mind. Hey, all power to ya. It's just hard to do both. Thanks to social engineers, justice warriors, media brainwashing and women's rights B.S., it is almost inevitable that society will keep going down the road it's going, and it ain't up ... it's down ... into the toilet. Don't believe (feminist) writers who spout otherwise. They only see the crab in the pot thinking it's cute, when really it's fighting for its life in the boiling water. Feminism is the boiling water, folks. Feminism is past its use to society and has now done more harm than good. There's a big difference between Feminism and femininity. No one needs feminism anymore. We do need more femininity and feminine women. We need each other, instead.

20. **Women say, "Where have all the good men gone?"** Men are saying the quality of women is so terrible today that they've left the building, bar, gym, mall, club, restaurant, online dating sites, etc., and they're off playing video games with their friends ... for good! Ladies, don't let them think that. Prove them otherwise by doing what's right.

21. **Men are supposed to be the protectors and providers. Women are supposed to be nurturers and caretakers.** For the most part, we're all hard wired from the day we are born as males and females. Unfortunately, feminists and the media are so obsessed with gender roles and political correctness B.S. that women fail

to see the forest from the trees. Reversing gender roles has only driven a wedge between men and women and created confusion in the dating world. Men don't want masculine women! Men want real, feminine women. Women who men can trust to be their wives and mothers of their children. Men want to retake the lead while women hold down the fort and socialize with their friends when the men are away. Sounds ideal, if you ask me, ladies. Again, you can do your own thing, but if you do, just know, you might be alone doing it for a long time. MY ADVICE: Avoid feminism. It will only poison your mind with lies, make you unattractive, and make you NOT girlfriend/wife material. Don't lose your femininity. There's nothing more unattractive to a man than a "masculine" woman who has a real disconnect with her feminine feelings and emotions.

22. **The only people having kids today are those who want them. Others have them by accident. Are you going to have yours by accident or planned with the one you love?** Don't put pressure on any man to have your baby. Look for one who will love you and want to start a family with you. Pressuring men like that only makes them not want you more. If having a family is important to you, at a certain point you just have to pick someone who expresses love and interest to procreate. Usually, everything else really does work out.

23. **If women don't watch out, what's the average guy gonna do? Get a passport, save up his money and travel to a few foreign countries with friends. What will they find? Fun, friendly girls with traditional values and potential wives.** If he doesn't go abroad, he'll simply ignore you here on your home turf. After dating foreign women, for many men, there's no returning to the locals (i.e., you, ladies). They find it's just not worth it. What's interesting is men with the means to travel to date foreign women. Guys don't prefer American girlfriends anymore. What's that say? If you're looking for Mr. Perfect, who

doesn't exist, and passing up the nice guys, well, take a cue from the ladies in other countries who American men desire and will go after with their saved income. Latin, European, African and Asian girls tend to be much nicer, youthful, healthier, thinner, curvy, dress more ladylike, and much more easy-going in terms of dating. They rarely look their age because of how well they take care of themselves. Sometimes, it's in the genes and I'm not talking *Levi*.

24. **In the end, success in relationships is best measured in your (and his) HAPPINESS together** not net worth, looks or anything else. Focus on finding a life partner and starting a family; someone you can build a life with. Look for quality conversation, mutual support, sharing of common interests, and respect for space and different interests.

25. **Ditch the *perfect guy* list. Go for 3-5 non-negotiables and 3-5 things you really need in your life.** Would he be a good dad? Think daddy material. Think husband material. Does he work? What is he passionate about? Also, think fun. Can you have fun with this man? Is he a good communicator? Is he patient? Does he take care of himself? Does he think of you often? Snag him before somebody else does.

26. **Make finding a man your main focus. Deviate from this strategy and you will waste time that you can never recover.** Once you do snag your man, don't stop living out the formula to KEEP HIM, which is dresses/skirts, heels, long hair, great skin, healthy lifestyle, etc.

27. **Don't take any of this personally, but do look at the big picture.** Remember, your mind has been hijacked and brainwashed into thinking like a maggot at the bottom of a garbage can. Get your head out of the pop culture boob tube and magazines that it's in and clean up, detox your mind,

and start looking for love, romance and a man whom you can grow old with. When you're old, if you haven't done these things, instead of hearing his voice in the morning say, *"Good morning, honey."* You'll instead hear, *"MEEOOOWWWW!"*

28. **The problem I see when I observe and listen closely to women when asked if they've ever been in a serious relationship and in love, most women ages 20-30 say, *"NO!"*** Wow, if they only knew what they were missing. Start appreciating men for who they are, what they've accomplished, what they can do for your love life, instead of demeaning them, kicking them to the curb for asking for that conversation with you. What's more important ... your phone, texting, chatting with your girlfriends or feeding your heart?

In closing, I hope I've given you plenty to think about and work on. You get the idea by now how important it is for you to WATCH OUT and do what's right and in alignment with nature, your heart, and not what's in your head or put there by social engineering, brainwashing media/feminists. Keep doing the things that you're already doing now, if you're single, otherwise you could find yourself still single at 30, 40, or 50+ years old unless it's a conscious choice to be alone. Considering dating a robot yourself? Marrying a sex toy? That is NOT a pretty picture by a long shot.

Now, granted, much of the problem does lie with men, too, who don't stand up to all the B.S. that's dumped on them on a daily basis. By nature, men are servants of the heart and want to work hard to make (you) happy. However, when they give up their freedoms and powers, would that make you happy? Men also ask themselves, what IS in it for them when they approach relationships with women today? Again, put yourself in his shoes. What is the risk/cost/reward factor with getting involved with a woman? How can you help lower that cost/risk assessment and increase the reward factor on an individual level? It's in your hands. You can do it. So? Do it!

There's something to say about too much freedom, too much choice, too much power. Have women been given too much freedom? Too much power? Too much of everything? Apparently not because some women are marching for more? How fat does a spoiled kid get when his parents feed him too much? How does your liver react when you drink too much alcohol? How do your lungs respond when you smoke too much? Are you getting the picture? More doesn't mean better, happier, or more successful? Sometimes, LESS is MORE. So, think about that.

Socially, today's woman is encouraged, empowered and maybe even expected to DO IT ALL / HAVE IT ALL. This, in itself, often causes more stress than it's worth. The SUPER WOMAN she's supposed to be never comes out. The SUPER MOM she's supposed to be is tired and stressed from work. Social norms tell her she is expected to run her home, succeed at work, raise perfect children, make her man happy, and be alive and pretty all at the same time. Whoa, talk about a tall order. To pull that off you have to be intelligent, educated, powerful and in control. Ladies, how about pick ONE AND A HALF of those qualities and perfect those? Such as, mom full-time, work from home (be with the kids) and make money. Screw career, unless it pays well, and replace job with home-based business if you can. There is so much opportunity out there today to make money from home. You don't have to go into work, again, unless it pays really well. Hey, go for it.

If you choose to do less, will you get more out of life? Probably. Stop trying to do it all and choose to do only a few things with a partner in crime (i.e., your future hubby), so you can enjoy life. Life is meant to be lived and enjoyed. Not consumed for the purpose of keeping corporate/global conglomerates in business. They're squeezing all of us for every nickle and dime we have, let alone our time.

Now, this isn't to say men don't need help to keep the relationship alive and humming either. They do not get a pass. Relationships are dance between two people. That's why I wrote *Laws Of The Bedroom*. It's just for men, for the benefit of the woman they love. Read it or listen to the audio and see why you want the *Laws* laid down for a lifetime of romantic benefits.

Ladies, changes always start from within. Before you ask men (or other women) to make changes, start with yourself. Adhere to what's inside this book and then share it with your best girlfriends and male friends as well. Then, try on these niceties on the men in your life. See how they (all) respond (kindly) in your direction. Then, you know, this book had your best interests at heart. Pursue that which your heart wants most, and don't stop, until you get it!

"We are taught you must blame your father, your sisters, your brothers, the school, the teachers - but never blame yourself. It's never your fault. But it's always your fault, because if you wanted to change you're the one who has got to change."

— Katharine Hepburn

RELATIONSHIP WEBSITE
Single? Looking for the <u>ONE</u> for you?

Single? Looking to meet other singles for a date, romance, fun, love, and/or a potential soul mate for LIFE? Then, check this out!

Bart has a very unique dating, relationship and matchmaking website for you? It's all based on the principles inside his books, **Find The One For Me**, *Laws Of The Bedroom*, **251+ Relationship Regrets**, **Watch Out Ladies**, and *B.S. The Book*. People at his website are looking for *real* relationships with meaning, depth and a future devoid of *B.S.* Using his books as a guide, members are able to jump right into conversations about what's really important to them when looking for the ONE for them!

  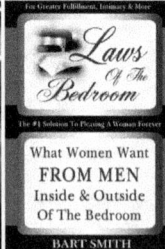 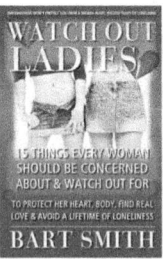 

With over 1,000+ pages and 100+ hours of real advice on dating, relationships, romance, love, sex, marriage, intimacy, parenting, and how to avoid all kinds of *B.S.* in your life! No dating website, app or matchmaking service has this much support material for its members, let alone this kind of guidance to help you FIND THE ONE for you!

FindTheOneForMe.com

SEMINARS & TELE-CLASSES
"Fireside Chats"

You'll definitely want to join Bart (by a virtual fireside) either on the telephone or live for one of his one-of-a-kind relationship talks if you really want to gain a true understanding and full effect of what his books and his messages have in store for you and the one for you.

Bart calls these talks *"Fireside Chats"* or *"Pillow Talk"* sessions because they're more than just a lecture on love and relationships. On the contrary, they're warm, personable, real, honest, direct, respectful *(to both sexes)* and yet comforting at the same time ... much like a "fireside chat" in your own home or "pillow talk" before turning in.

Listen to Bart's particular brand of conversation with deep regard for the subject matter he covers, which is intentionally designed to be uniquely informative and extremely enriching. Visit Bart's website for more information on how to register and attend one of his events by telephone or live at an event coming soon.

BartSmithBooks.com/events

GET THE AUDIO VERSION

Don't settle for just the written version of Bart's books when you can listening to the audio versions of **Watch Out Ladies**, **Find The One For Me**, **251+ Dating & Relationship Regrets**, **Laws Of The Bedroom** and *B.S. The Book* in **AUDIO** format?

Why is the **audio version** so effective for learning this material? For starters, you can **listen to Bart's books** wherever you are and on virtually any device. Just imagine relaxing and focusing on Bart's recorded material with just the right tonality, emphasis, and inflection for the maximum learning experience. For a real treat, dim the lights, light a candle or two, pour a glass of wine or other beverage, grab a few of Bart's world famous chocolate chip cookies (BartsCookies.com), and hit the PLAY button!

Then, lay your head back on the pillow, couch or sofa and close your eyes and listen to this material being read to you. Do you commute? Turn up your speakers and listen while you drive to/from work. Take advantage of all that road time and enjoy the commute. Just imagine what you'll learn during rush hour and dream confidently about not experiencing so many regrets going forward.

Bart's audio complements his books. Both are MUST-HAVES! Listening to the audio version of any of Bart's books present an unparalleled learning experience. Not only does Bart cover every parameter you need to know about, but he also emphasizes particular areas you may want to learn more about (in the audio) where your life and relationships are concerned. Sample before you buy. Go to:

BartSmithBooks.com/audio

BART'S COOKBOOK

WHO'S HUNGRY?

HOW TO MAKE BART'S "WORLD FAMOUS" PIZZA, SALAD, OMELETTE, PARTY SMOOTHIE, PAD THAI DISH & MORE

BART SMITH   BartsKitchen.com

Who's Hungry? is Bart's personal menu for what he serves up at home when it comes to **breakfast**, **lunch**, and **dinner**, as well as, fun stuff like his world famous **party smoothie**!

Every single man/woman, and every family in America and around the world; anyone who likes delicious (home-cooked) food, anyone who wants to learn how to cook, lose weight, and/or learn a few new tricks in the kitchen or dishes to add to their current list of meals they currently make ... BART'S COOKBOOK is a MUST-HAVE in your kitchen!

"Well, I've had Bart's tortellini and salmon, his pizza, his salad, his soft tacos, smoothies, fried rice and his Yakisoba stir-fry noodles with mixed seafood, and other dishes. When I brought friends over to enjoy these dishes they were blown away at how fast and fun Bart whipped 'em up. Speechless, he left them! What's more, I assisted him when he made over 30 PITCHERS of his world famous party smoothie at a party. He stole the show! Everyone came back for seconds, thirds and fourth cups of his party potion! His cookies also disappeared faster than we could say, 'Where'd they go?' Bart, you rock, always!" – Gale G., Huntington Bch., CA

BartsCookbook.com + BartsKitchen.com

OTHER RELATIONSHIP BOOKS BY BART

FIND THE ONE FOR ME
Insights, Wisdom & Real Advice
For Finding The ONE For You

I wrote this book for singles and those in relationships on their way out! Whether you're looking for love online or offline, **Find The One For Me** has everything you need to help navigate the world of liars, cheats, crazies, sex hungry maniacs, and **B.S.** so you too can find that ideal person worth spending time with, interacting with, securing and eventually choosing him/her for you to live with and/or marry. **Find The One For Me** is your bible for navigating the jungle of love and hearts. All you have to do is open up this book to find 180 + topics never covered in other relationship books. I can only hope this huge collection of insights, findings, and words of wisdom can help you find that special someone who's also looking ... **for you!**

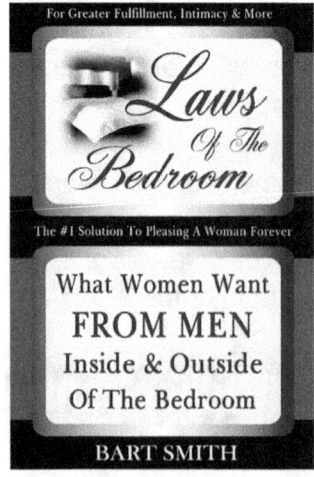

Laws Of The Bedroom
What Women Want From Men Inside & Outside Of The Bedroom

I wrote this book for men to learn more about what women really want from them, both inside and outside of the bedroom. From what I can tell, women are not getting treated the way they should be able to expect when it comes to healthy/happy/nurturing relationships with the men they're dating, engaged to or even married to. For example, men are not giving women the right kind of attention, emotional care, mental stimulation, or even enough time to become aroused (before making love), let alone the right touch to excite a woman's spiritual and deeply rooted passion that she naturally and instinctively *craves! Laws Of The Bedroom* ™ is the only book men really need that shares specific insights into a woman's desires and what men should say and do to attract, please and sustain a relationship with a woman ... FOREVER!

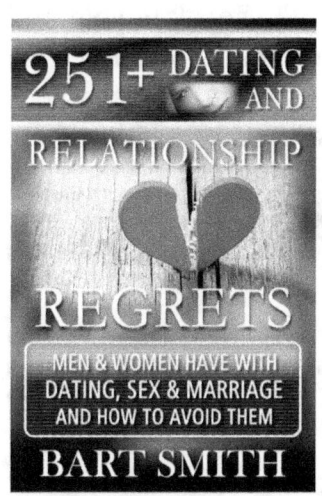

251+ DATING, SEX & RELATIONSHIP REGRETS
Men & Women Have With Dating, Sex & Marriage & How To Avoid Them

You'll love this book for what it can do for you, which is, help you avoid 251+ dating, sex, marriage and relationship regrets others have had. Why reinvent the wheel? Why go through what others have experienced, especially if it turned out bad? Don't you want to live your life with the one you're with and avoid as much heartache, trouble, strife, regret, or unexpected/undesired consequences from the decisions you (or the two of you) make? I would! That's why I wrote it!

Overall, this book stands out from all the rest as one book everyone in the world should read. Whether you're single or in a relationship. Everyone can benefit from the regrets people have had so they don't repeat them too. This book simply makes you wisen up or else suffer the consequences. You know what I mean?

Keeping a copy of this book around and rereading it from time to time will help remind you (as it does myself) what we should be watching out for so we don't regret anything by mistake.

BART'S COOKIES

If you really want to know what it's like to be in a heaven-sent, orgasmically addictive, blissfully overloaded state of mind in your relationship with the ONE you love, then try **Bart's world famous chocolate chip cookies**. Did you know that Bart also commercially bakes the world's best dark chocolate chip, milk chocolate chip, white chocolate chip, white chocolate chip with macadamia nuts, peanut butter with milk chocolate chip and his favorite ... milk+dark chocolate chip combo. Yes, and even gluten-free cookies as well? All flavors have no preservatives. Check it out along with 300+ cookie reviews by visiting:

BartsCookies.com + iLoveBartsCookies.com

"My cookies are always freshly baked, soft, yet crunchy, and chewy, and the ultimate of chocolate orgams in your mouth like never before experienced.

Milk+Dark Chocolate Chip "Combo" Cookie (Guaranteed To Blow Your Mind!)

White Chocolate Chip with Macadamia Nuts

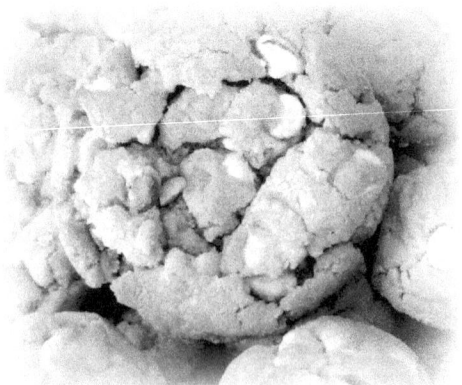

MEET THE AUTHOR

BART SMITH

Watch Out Ladies author, BART SMITH, shares 30+ years of full-time observations, research, life experience, and conversations with men and women in the areas of life, love, relationships, dating, sex, marriage and FINDING THE ONE for you.

His hope with this book? To help encourage every woman to take a serious look deep inside herself as to her behaviors and decisions she makes that can, and often do, have consequences regarding her present and future love life. His advice? Choose wisely, think twice, consider the pros/cons of any decision you make, both short-term and long-term, so you wind up winning with someone and not losing, on your own and alone as you get older. By sharing decades worth of sound advice, insight and explanation about current and destructive trends that affect both men and women, proven guidelines to help keep women's hearts and bodies safe, heartfelt suggestions on living life, and other advice, women who are single today can look forward to FINDING THE ONE for them sooner, rather than later, or not at all.

For more than three decades, Bart continues to hold true to the ideals he shares with others. He's also witnessed significant improvement in the lives of those he has spent time with, whether one-on-one or in group format. Much like *Laws Of The Bedroom*, Bart's content is grounded in real life experience. He makes you feel there really is hope for love and romance in this crazy whacked out world, that he understands what yoWow, what more could you want someone to do/be for you? Bart does all that and more inside **Watch Out Ladies** and all his books.